ESSENTIAL STRATEGIES

for WORD STUDY

Effective Methods for Improving Decoding, Spelling, and Vocabulary

Timothy Rasinski & Jerry Zutell

SCHOLASTIC

New York • Toronto • London • Auckland • Sydney
Mexico City • New Delhi • Hong Kong • Buenos Aires

Editor: Lois Bridges

Production editor: Gloria Pipkin

Cover design: Jorge J. Namerow

Interior design: Holly Grundon

Copy editor: David Klein

ISBN-13: 978-0-545-10333-6

ISBN 10: 0-545-10333-9

Copyright © 2010 by Timothy Rasinski and Jerry Zutell

All rights reserved. Published by Scholastic Inc.

Printed in the U.S.A.

2 3 4 5 6 7 8 9 10   40   17 16 15 14 13 2 11

Table *of* Contents

Introduction

Part I: Examining Word Structure

Part II: Exploring Word Meanings

Table *of* **Contents**

Part III: Extending Word Knowledge

dedication
and acknowledgments

We dedicate this book to the two people whose words have meant the most to us throughout our adult lives—our wives, Kathy and Kate. Kathy and Kate—as the songwriter Johnny Mercer wrote, "You're just too marvelous, too marvelous for words . . .!"

We wish to acknowledge those people whose thoughts, research, and writing on word study have educated us, provided us with insight, and inspired us to understand word study as an integral part of the school literacy experience. In this volume we particularly drew upon the work of Camille Blachowicz and Connie Obrochta, Mary Jo Fresch and Aileen Wheaton, Isabel Beck, Pat Cunningham, and Zaner-Bloser's *Word Wisdom*. We have particularly benefited from our interactions with our close colleagues and friends: Nancy Padak, Evangeline Newton, Rick Newton, Pat Scharer, Mary Jo Fresch, and Marytherese Croarkin. Edmund Henderson and his students from the University of Virginia and Edgar Dale and Joseph O'Rourke from The Ohio State University deserve special recognition as mentors and colleagues who built traditions of scholarship and educational practice in the study of words to which we proudly belong. We salute these and the many other scholars and educators who dared to speak about word study when spelling, phonics, and vocabulary instruction were not considered popular nor particularly important.

We also acknowledge the fabulous support, tireless and sincere encouragement, and professional insight of our editor, Lois Bridges. Lois, this book would not have been possible without you. Ironically, words cannot sufficiently express how indebted we are to you. Thank you.

Introduction

This book is about word study in the elementary and middle grades. You may be wondering to yourself, **"Just what is word study? Is it phonics? Is it spelling? Is it vocabulary instruction—teaching students the meaning of words?"** Well, in three words, the answers to your questions are yes, yes, and yes.

What Is Word Study?

Word study is about the direct study and exploration of words. In school we typically think of phonics, spelling, and vocabulary as three distinct parts of the curriculum—we often separate materials for each area. But think about how words are usually organized inside your head. Do you think you have a separate area of your brain devoted to the sound of words, a separate area for the spelling of words, and a separate area for the meaning of words? That seems highly unlikely. When we store words in our brain, the sound, spelling, and meaning are usually consolidated. When we view a word on the printed page, we access the sound, spelling, and meaning simultaneously and immediately.

With this understanding of consolidated word knowledge, we believe that the best way to approach the teaching of words is not in piecemeal fashion, as has been done in the past, but in an integrated way where the spelling, sound, and meaning of words are areas of focus at the same time. When we teach children how to sound out a word, we also have a great opportunity to discuss how the word is spelled and what it means. Word study, then, is simply the part of the school curriculum where we explore the full nature of words with students simultaneously—sound, spelling, and meaning. Not only is such an approach more efficient for students and teachers, it also provides opportunities for higher levels of engagement and interest. Word study and instruction in words can and should be an interesting and engaging part of the school curriculum. With this book, we hope to offer you the tools to make that happen.

Why Is Word Study Important?

It makes simple yet compelling sense that the ability to decode and understand words is essential to success in reading. Readers cannot begin to apply comprehension strategies until they have some degree of mastery in word recognition and vocabulary. In the late 1990s, Congress appointed a panel of experts to review the research on reading and learning to read. After a thorough and strict review of research, this group, known as the National Reading Panel (2000), concluded that there is a strong body of empirical evidence that direct instruction in phonics (word decoding) and vocabulary (word meanings) are important factors in learning to read. The panel did not endorse a single approach to the teaching of reading, only that direct instruction in the decoding and meaning of words will improve students' reading.

Spelling, in our view, is the flip side of decoding. In fact, some experts call it encoding. Our own research (Zutell, 1992; Zutell & Rasinski, 1989) has found a strong relationship between students' ability to spell and their proficiency in reading. Students who can take an oral form of a word and produce the correct written form (spell) are very likely to be able to take the written form of a word and produce the oral form (decoding). So we view spelling as an extension of phonics. When we work with students on how to spell words, we are also working with them on their ability to decode words.

Clearly, the job of teaching words is a challenge. Not only do some words in English have remarkably odd spelling patterns, varied pronunciations, or several meanings, there are also plenty of words in English that students need to learn. It has been estimated that there are more words in English than in any other language in the world (Rasinski, et al, 2008). Moreover, students must acquire many of those words. Bauman, Kame'enui, and Ash (2003) concluded that, beginning in third grade, the average student adds approximately 3,000 words per year to his or her personal vocabulary!

Word knowledge is essential for word decoding and reading comprehension, as well as oral communication and writing. In our own reading clinics at Kent State University and Ohio State University, we routinely have seen evidence of the importance of words. Elementary and middle school students come to our programs with problems in reading. When we take a closer look at their reading, we find that in many cases they have difficulty in decoding (and spelling) words. In other cases, students have difficulty in determining the meaning of words that they can successfully decode. (What good is it to be able to decode a word but not know its meaning? That essentially makes the word a nonsense word for students.) In many cases, students show evidence of difficulty in both decoding and vocabulary. Knowing this, we work with students on word decoding and vocabulary using the very methods described in this book, and not only do decoding and vocabulary improve, but, more important, so do reading comprehension, reading achievement, and motivation for reading.

Word study is important because it improves reading and writing. (Have you ever seen a writing rubric that didn't include word choice and spelling as criteria for good writing?) And although most of us would readily agree that word study is important, the approaches offered in the past have not been terribly engaging for students or teachers. Often, word study has been little more than lists of words students must memorize, committing to memory both the spelling and meaning of the selected words. Word study workbooks and/or worksheets have been another common approach: students simply complete required workbook pages over the course of a week, get the corrections back, and are "rewarded" with another set of pages to complete. None of these approaches can be characterized as effective, engaging, or even reasonable, if we expect students to master 3,000 words per year. Indeed, to have any sort of real instructional impact—and come close to that 3,000-word goal—these approaches would need to present students with 75 words per week over the course of a school year. Unfortunately, it's these dry approaches to word study that have convinced many students (and adults) to regard the study of words as boring. Don't get us wrong. The teachers and school leaders who employ such methods do so with the very best of intentions; however, good intentions do not necessarily add up to good instruction.

This book is about making word study engaging and effective. Word study should be interesting. We hope the methods in this book will allow that to happen in your own teaching, regardless of what subject area you specialize in or what grade level you teach.

When Should Word Study Happen?

We think that word study is so important that there should be a designated part of each day devoted to it. Many schools have adopted a four- or five-block language arts curriculum where one block may be devoted to guided reading, one to writing, one to fluency, one to independent reading, and so on. Whether you do four, five, or six blocks, one of those blocks needs to be word study.

How much time per day should be devoted to word study? In most classrooms that employ a four- or five-block approach, approximately 30 minutes is devoted to each block. We feel that 30 minutes per day would be an appropriate length of time to devote to word study. Now, if you work in a middle school where only one 50-minute period per day is devoted to reading and language arts, then you are going to have to adjust. Perhaps you can only devote 10–15 minutes per day or 30 minutes three times per week to word study. Regardless of how you schedule it, word study needs to be a regular and recurring component of your reading and language arts curriculum. Remember that during this period the goal of word study is to study words directly and intensively—how they are pronounced, how they are spelled, and what they mean—in an integrated manner.

Word study can and should also happen in your content-area instruction. It is in science, math, social studies, and the other content areas that students encounter academic words—words unique to a particular academic discipline. These words are particularly important because knowledge of them is critical to students' understanding of the content and to their ability to independently read and understand content reading material.

Commit yourself to the study of words with students in your content-area instruction. Before, during, and after lessons and readings, devote time to introducing and reinforcing the words that are essential to understanding the content. Obviously, you won't have as much time to give to word study as you might in your word study block; nevertheless, finding 5–10 minutes at the right time for examining and playing with academic words can make all the difference between deep and limited understanding. Many of the methods presented in this book are powerful tools for promoting deep analysis and understanding of words found in content-area instruction.

In addition to the dedicated time each day devoted to word study, as well as time for word study in all of your content areas, be aware of those teachable moments when word study may take only a minute or two, but because the words you are teaching during that moment are both visible and pronounced for students, they will learn them, and learn them well, in that short period of time. Many teachers have a word of the day, a time in which a new word or two is introduced at the beginning of each day. Current events always provide the opportunity to examine new words. When the president of the United States visits the leader of another country, the meeting is often called a *summit*. Here's a great chance to talk about *summit*, put it on the Word Wall, and use it throughout the day. When an outbreak of the *flu* threatens a *pandemic*, you might wonder aloud to your students what a *pandemic* is and how the *flu* came to be given that odd name, then look up *flu* and *pandemic* in an online dictionary. What you will find will be enough to present the following information to your students:

Flu, a shortened version of *influenza*, a viral disease of the respiratory system. The name *influenza* means influence—originally it was thought that influenza outbreaks were caused by the influence of the stars.

Pandemic: A disease spread across a large part of the world. It is derived from two Greek words: *pan,* meaning all, and *dem,* meaning people. Pandemic is a disease that has the potential to spread to all people of a country or the world.

From these two Greek derivations you can expand to words such as *Pan-African studies, Pan-American games, panorama, panacea, democracy, demographics, democrat,* etc. All of these words, and more, can be added to the day's Word Wall. In a matter of minutes, you have introduced your students to at least ten words, and you have given them tools, through the Greek derivations, to unlock the meaning, sound, and spelling of many more words. Great teachers need to be able to pounce on teachable moments.

What Words Should You Teach?

This is really a tough question to answer. It would be nice if we could present you with a list of words that we absolutely know that students must learn at every grade level. We have provided you with a few very small lists of words and word parts that we think are important, but we will not go further than that. You see, the words you should teach depend on your students' stages of development, the books and other materials your students will be reading, the content you will be covering in other subject areas, and even the current events in the world and your local communities. Moreover, words are always being added to English, and some words that may have been important at one time have lost their importance. So trying to come up with one list of words that is appropriate for all students for all time is like trying to hit a moving target; it is very tough indeed.

We feel it is essential that you (and your students) become the deciders of a good number of the words that you need to teach. You and your students know the words that your students don't know, and you should have a pretty good idea of the words they need to know. As you preview passages your students will be reading and content you will be covering in various areas of your curriculum, make note of the words, phrases, and other written expressions that you think are essential for students to understand, or the content and the words that you think are most likely to cause your students difficulty with decoding, spelling, and understanding. Keep a list of these words in a notebook or spreadsheet. These are the words you should be teaching! These are the words most closely connected to students' own reading, learning, and living. Ask students to do much the same. It is important for them to develop an awareness of those words that they need to know. All of this takes a matter of minutes every day. You have a great sense for finding those words that you need to teach. And once you have done this for a school year, you have a solid foundation for at least some of the words that need to be part of your word study program in future years.

How Should You Develop Your Word Study Program?

We hope you will use word study in all the ways we just described—in a daily word study component or block of your language arts period, in your content-area instruction, and in those delicious teachable moments that happen almost every day. Your next question, we suppose, is "OK, I buy into word study, but how do I create a word study program that is not just a bunch of worksheets or word lists for memorization?"

We're glad you asked. That is where this book comes in. There is no one best way to teach words to students. Good teaching depends on your goal for instruction, the nature of the words you wish to teach, the grade and development level of your students, and your own style of teaching. We do recognize the value of *research-based* student textbooks to support student learning. In fact, we are textbook authors ourselves and have incorporated many of the activities in this book into our published materials. However, we are also firm believers that teachers should develop their own instructional routines for word study. In this book, we present 30 instructional approaches for teaching students about words. Some of the strategies are more appropriate for some grade levels than for others, some for general word learning, and some are more appropriate for content-area word instruction. Nevertheless, these strategies have all been shown to be effective through empirical research and/or classroom and clinical implementation.

In a sense, these strategies represent a set of tools that you can choose from in designing a program of word study that works best for you and your students. As you read through this book, ask yourself which strategies appeal to your own sense of instruction and your own teaching situation. Fit them into a weekly instructional routine that you wish to follow in your word study program. You may choose two or three strategies to employ on Mondays, Wednesdays, and Fridays, and two others for Tuesdays and Thursdays. For your content-area word study, you may choose three strategies that you will learn deeply and apply whenever the need arises.

When we invest in and take ownership of our own instruction, we are more likely to work hard to make that instruction work. So after you read this book, the challenge falls to you: What strategies will you choose, and how will you use them in designing word study for your students? We think you will also enjoy what we have to share. Word study should be fun and engaging for you and your students. We sincerely hope that this book of strategies and activities will be the starting point for making word study an integral and dynamic part of your language arts and content-area curricula. It's deserving of nothing less.

Why Is a Developmental Perspective Important?

We believe that you will find the activities we share with you in the following pages not only engaging and enjoyable but also powerful tools for advancing your students' word knowledge. Still, to maximize their instructional benefits, you will need to make choices about which activities to use when, and what content to cover with those activities. We are confident that your professional knowledge, your understanding of your students' interests and abilities, and your skill at observation and assessment will inform these choices so your students receive highly effective instruction.

An essential part of your professional knowledge is your understanding of the developmental nature of word learning, so we think it important to briefly review what research has told us about how students learn about words. We expect that you are familiar with many of these ideas already, since there is a substantial research literature supporting them and many recent professional resources describing these findings and detailing their application to instruction. For your convenience, we have included a brief list of professional books about the developmental nature of word knowledge (see p. 18). You may find it helpful to use one of these resources to either develop or refresh your knowledge, though you may well find the information below enough of a review to select and apply the activities described in these pages to your students' best benefit.

Here are some elements we consider essential in understanding word learning as a developmental process:

1. English orthography (another word for the writing system) is complex but systematic. English is fundamentally an alphabetic orthography built on letter-sound (reading) and sound-letter (spelling) correspondences. But these are not absolute. There are also other layers of organization that include pattern (how letter combinations are related to pronunciation and spelling), meaning (words with the same pronunciations are spelled differently to represent different meanings—e.g., homophones like *sail* and *sale*; or parts of words may be pronounced differently but are spelled the same to represent the same meaning—e.g., the consistent *-ed* spelling in *missed*, *bowled*, and *wanted* to represent past tense), and history or word origin (pronunciation changes over time may affect alphabetic relationships—e.g., the now silent *k* in *knight* was originally pronounced; words adopted from other languages may retain the letter-sound correspondences from that language—e.g., the three different pronunciations of *ch-* in *child* (Old English), *chef* (French), and *chorus* (Greek) yet the "ch" pronunciation of the *c* in the Italian-derived *cello*).

Thus good readers and spellers may benefit from considering not only how a word sounds, but also how it looks, what it means, and where it comes from in unlocking its pronunciation, spelling, or meaning.

2. There are strong relationships between word learning for reading and word learning for spelling. Traditionally reading and spelling have been separate and often unconnected parts of the elementary grade curriculum, taught at different times and often with completely different materials. Yet in our own work (Zutell, 1992; Zutell & Rasinski, 1989) we found high correlations between student ability to read words accurately and quickly, both in isolation and in context, and student performance on a developmental spelling inventory. For the most part, students learn to read individual words before they learn to spell them, but better spellers are better readers. We found almost no students who were good spellers who were not good at recognizing words accurately and easily. We came to the conclusion that an underlying construct of word knowledge governs word learning for both reading and spelling.

This conclusion has important implications for instruction because it suggests that an integrated program of word study makes more sense than treating phonics, spelling, and vocabulary as separate, unconnected parts of the curriculum.

3. Learning to read and to spell involves both memorization and conceptualization. It is clear that students learn many words by seeing and saying them accurately and often. Thus word familiarity/frequency does have an important benefit. But as learners become more proficient, they also form concepts about how words work. They become aware of possible patterns and more complex relationships. This can be seen in the sequence of spelling development in which, for example, all other things being equal, short vowel words are learned more easily than long vowel words. It can also be seen in how students' misspellings change over time, so that a word like *stepped* may be first misspelled as SP, then STAPT, then STEPT, then STEPED before being spelled correctly. Each change in spelling reveals the understanding of a new word feature, including full sound-letter matching, control over short *e*, the constancy of –*ed* for past tense, and consonant doubling. Moreover, memory and concept development support each other. The more words with a particular pattern or feature that a learner knows, the easier it will be to recognize and learn that pattern or feature. On the other hand, once a pattern or feature is learned, the easier it is to learn new words with that pattern or feature. Concept formation provides the "glue" that helps word forms "stick" in memory.

4. Learning words, and about words, is a developmental process in which students go through specific phases of word learning and stages of spelling development. The chart below, created by Jerry and his co-author Sandy McCormick (McCormick & Zutell, 2101), is based in the research in this area. It provides names and brief descriptions for each phase and stage. The side-by-side structure shows the clear parallels between these two aspects of development. Note that as students move from phase to phase and stage to stage, their word knowledge changes both quantitatively and qualitatively. They not only learn more words as they move to higher phases and stages, but how they attack words and how they attempt to spell them also change.

Comparing Phases of Word Learning and Stages of Spelling Development	
Word Learning	**Spelling Development**
Pre-Alphabetic • Minimal number of words in isolation read correctly • Letter-sound relationships not used • Some graphic cues (word length, shape) used, not always consistently	**Emergent: Pre-Alphabetic** • Scribbles or apparently random letter/number strings used to represent message
Partial-Alphabetic • Some high-frequency and familiar words learned "by sight" • Beginning and ending consonant letter-sound cues sometimes used for word recognition	**Late Emergent/Early Letter Name** • Beginning, then beginning and ending consonants used to represent single-syllable words • Vowels represented only occasionally, especially in long-vowel words

chart continued on next page

Essential Strategies for Word Study | **Introduction**

Comparing Phases of Word Learning and Stages of Spelling Development

Word Learning	Spelling Development
Full-Alphabetic • High-frequency and familiar words learned more easily • Initially words decoded letter-by-letter, moving left to right across the word • More letter-sound correspondences learned, and more easily	**Letter-Name or Phonetic** • Each phoneme in single-syllable words represented in a logical way • Names of letters often used as source of information to represent sounds in words • Short vowel words often misspelled using letter-name substitutions • Minimal use of vowel markers and silent letters
Consolidated-Alphabetic • Letter combinations or spelling patterns used for word recognition • New words identified by analogy to known patterns • Knowledge and use of letter combinations lead to easier recognition of multisyllabic words	**Within-Word Pattern** • Most short-vowel, single-syllable words and high- frequency words spelled correctly • Long-vowel markers used, but only gradually used consistently • Initially silent-e sometimes used on short-vowel words • Minimal use of double consonants in two-syllable words except for high-frequency ones
Automatic • Stable control over large sight vocabulary • Variety of strategies used successfully to identify unknown words	**Syllable Juncture and Affixes** • Most regular single-syllable words and high-frequency words spelled correctly • Consonant-doubling and e-drop patterns learned gradually • Unstressed vowels in multisyllabic words spelled by "sound"
	Derivational Constancy • Consonant-doubling and e-drop patterns at word ending used correctly • Consonant-doubling at prefix-root boundary learned gradually • Constancy of vowel spellings in multisyllabic words from the same root learned gradually • Extensive spelling vocabulary including multisyllabic words acquired

Three Professional Books That Address Word Knowledge

Words Their Way: Word Study for Phonics, Vocabulary, and Spelling Instruction by Donald R. Bear, Marcia Invernizzi, Shane Templeton, and Francine Johnston (2007). This popular resource, now in its fourth edition, employs a developmental, hands-on approach and includes a variety of word sorts and games.

Teaching and Assessing Spelling: A Practical Approach That Strikes the Balance Between Whole-Group and Individualized Instruction by Mary Jo Fresch and Aileen Wheaton (2002). A Spelling Knowledge Inventory provides an analysis of each student's spelling knowledge and supports whole-class, small-group, and individualized instruction at each stage of development.

Word Journeys: Assessment-Guided Phonics, Spelling, and Vocabulary Instruction by Kathy Ganske (2002). The Developmental Spelling Analysis allows teachers to assess students' spelling development and knowledge of key orthographic features and to tailor word study to their individual needs and strengths. Reproducible forms for administering the DSA are included in the appendix.

 5. You can use your knowledge of these phases and stages in combination with observations of your students' reading and writing behaviors to select content and activities that best match their instructional needs. We know that students learn best when they are working with materials at their appropriate instructional level. In word study, we often focus instruction on those patterns students are "using but confusing" within their developmental level (Invernizzi, Abouzeid, & Gill, 1994). Students are "using but confusing" when they have control over a particular pattern in a good number of familiar words but struggle to spell the pattern when they are stretched to apply it to words they are less familiar with.

For example, in the Within-Word Pattern stage of spelling development (see p. 17), students gradually master the marking patterns for long vowel words. As they figure out the differences between short and long vowel spelling patterns, they tend to spell most long vowel words with the vowel-consonant-e pattern (e.g., *hope*, *game*) correctly. They may also spell well-known vowel-vowel-consonant words (e.g., *boat*, *rain*) accurately. However, less visually familiar vowel-vowel-consonant words (e.g., *soak*, *claim*) may well be spelled with a silent-e (e.g., SOKE, CLAME). If you had students who exhibited these behaviors, you, as an informed and observant teacher, might construct word study activities, for example, a set of word sorts (see pp. 39–42) through which your students could compare and contrast different long vowel spelling patterns.

Each of the activities described in the following pages is consistent with a child-centered, constructive, developmental view of word learning. We believe that if you use the five essential elements outlined above to guide you in the selection and application of word study activities, you will provide your students with the best possible word study instruction.

Examining Word Structure

The activities in Part I focus on careful study of how words are built. **They examine the relationships among pronunciation, meaning and letters, letter combinations, and meaning units: prefixes, base words/roots, and suffixes.** We explore other word formations, including clipping and combining words, making words from the names of proper names of people, places, and things, and adopting and adapting words from other languages through the study of word histories and origins.

Directed Spelling Thinking Activity (DSTA)

What: The Directed Spelling Thinking Activity (DSTA) (Zutell, 1996) is a multiday lesson framework for delivering spelling instruction that challenges students to think deeply about the nature of the spelling of words. The steps and procedures were built to parallel those in the Directed Reading-Thinking Activity (DR-TA) developed by literacy expert Russell Stauffer (1975). Stauffer believed that reading instruction should more directly engage students in actively forming hypotheses and testing them against the information collected during reading. The DSTA also relies on this hypothesis-testing approach to learning.

Why: Learning a large, comprehensive spelling vocabulary requires more than rote practice and memorization of a list of words on which students are tested (usually on Fridays). The DSTA was developed to provide a more active approach to spelling instruction that engages students in thinking about word/spelling patterns and forming concepts about how words work, thus the inclusion of the word *thinking* in its title.

Who: The DSTA is appropriate for large- and small-group instruction across the grades in which spelling is formally taught. Typically, teachers begin using the DSTA in late first or early second grade, when students have acquired a significant enough sight vocabulary that they can read the words they need to learn to spell. It can also be adapted to individual tutoring situations.

When and Where: Since the DSTA was developed as an alternative to traditional memorization-based spelling frameworks, it is best employed during regular spelling instruction time. You should plan for 15–20 minutes a day for a minimum of five days (the typical spelling instruction cycle). However, that time can be expanded depending upon the number and nature of words to be learned. As with many instructional models, the cycle begins with high teacher input and moves toward small-group and independent work that can be done at various times during the school day. The DSTA is appropriate for learning sets of words with specific orthographic/spelling patterns that contrast with other patterns (e.g., short vowel words vs. long vowel words). It is not usually appropriate when studying lists of high-frequency words or words on special topics (e.g., days of the week, color words, etc.).

How: Here are the major steps in using the DSTA:

- **Word Selection.** You select two to four word patterns to study and 12–20 words matched to the patterns. Some "exception words" are often included. Ideally, students should be able to read all the words but only spell about half correctly. Alternatively, words may come from across one or more basal spelling lessons.

- **Pretest.** A traditional pretest format is used: Words are presented in random order. You say the word, use it in a sentence, and say the word again. Students spell the word on their test paper. No strict time limit is set, and students may ask for the word to be repeated.

- **Discussion.** Spellings are not corrected immediately. Before you reveal the correct spelling for each word, you lead a brief discussion in which students volunteer their spellings (written on a whiteboard or chart paper) and discuss the reasons guiding their attempts. To stimulate discussion, you might ask: a) "What were you thinking when you spelled the word that way?" b) "What other word(s) on the list so far are like this one?" or c) "How would a word spelled this way be pronounced?" At the end of the discussion, the students put into words what they think the "rules" are for spelling these kinds of words.

- **Teacher Modeled/Assisted Word Sort.** Using a pocket chart or magnetic board, you model how to sort the words into columns (see the directions for Word Sorts, pp. 39–40), talking through your decisions and gradually incorporating the group into the decision-making process. At the end of the sort, you and your students develop a more explicit and precise statement of the "rules" or patterns explaining how the words are spelled.

◆ **Brainstorming and/or Word Hunting.** Students can add their own examples to the columns and/or you instruct them to search a selection of their readings and writings and/or their word journals to find other examples of words that follow the previously described "rules." At this point, you and/or your students determine a final set of words to be studied from the original list and newly found words, either by individual or for the group.

◆ **Practice.** Students then work in pairs, small groups, or individually in a variety of ways to practice their words. This might involve a) paired word sorts in which students work with a partner helping each other sort their common and individual words (see pp. 39–42 for a fuller discussion of word sorting), b) flip folders (see pp. 116–118), c) games in which advancing, scoring, or another measure of success is determined by students' ability to spell and pronounce words correctly (see pp. 129–130), or d) practice tests.

◆ **Final Assessment and Evaluation.** You, an aide, a volunteer, or a peer administers a post-test, using either individual words or dictated sentences. Final tests may also include unstudied examples of the patterns to see if students can apply what they've learned. Assessments are scored for the percentage of total study words correct and for control of the patterns being studied. (Note: students may spell a word incorrectly but still spell the pattern under study correctly, e.g., SKARED for *scared* when studying *r*-controlled vowels.)

Here's an outline of a DSTA that Elise Schille did with one group of her fifth-grade students. Elise noticed that members of this group struggled at times with *dg* words. They would usually spell high-frequency examples like *badge*, *edge*, and *bridge* correctly, but they sometimes stumbled over less frequent examples like *budget*, *ledger*, and *gadget*, either omitting the *d* or using *gg* rather than the *dg* combination. These students might also occasionally fail to double the *g* in words like *beggar* and *nugget*. She decided to contrast the *dg* pattern used in short vowel, soft *g* words (e.g., *bridge*) with the *gg* pattern in short vowel, hard *g* words (e.g., *beggar*) and with the vowel-*g*-*e*/*i* patterns used in long vowel, soft *g* words (e.g., *cages*).

Elise began with a brief test of 12 words that either follow one of these patterns or are exceptions to them. The list consisted of *pledge, nugget, wager, badger, slugger, fidget, manage, lodger, scrooge, stagger, refrigerator,* and *smudge*. After the test, students shared their spellings of each word, one by one. As she expected, on average her students spelled about 60% of the words correctly, but different students misspelled different words. As students offered incorrect spellings, Elise guided them to examine the relationships between pronunciations and spellings using the questions suggested above: a) "What were you thinking when you spelled the word that way?" b) "What other word(s) on the list so far are like this one?" c) "How would a word spelled this way be pronounced?" For example, when a student misspelled *fidget* as FIGET, Elise suggested he compare the pronunciation of the word, and specifically the *g*, to each of the first three words on the list, which were by then written correctly on the board. He quickly recognized that in this part of the word, *fidget* is similar to *pledge* and so should be spelled with *dg*. In another instance, Elise asked a student how she thought her spelling, LOGGER, for *lodger*, would be pronounced. The student recognized that it would be pronounced with a hard *g* pronunciation and agreed that the spelling should be *dg,* as in *pledge, badger,* and *fidget*, which had already been discussed. When they had discussed all the words and presented the correct spellings, the students came to some conclusions about the words they had examined. They concluded that: a) *g* could have a "soft" or "hard" pronunciation, b) sometimes soft *g* might be spelled *dg*, sometimes just *g*, and c) the hard *g* pronunciation was usually spelled with a double *g* in words with suffixes attached. The discussion indicated they were not yet quite sure about all the relationships between pronunciation and spelling patterns.

The next day, Elise began the lesson by asking members of the group what they remembered from the prior test and discussion. With only a little prompting they were able to restate the general conclusions they had reached the day before. In preparation for the lesson, Elise had constructed a word sort using the test words and some others. It consisted of five categories (see below). (She had added a single-syllable, final hard *g* category to round out the comparison, though she had considered the words in it too simple for the earlier test.)

DSTA Word Sort for Hard and Soft *g*

Final g	-dg-	-gg-	-Vge-	?
brag	pledge	nugget	wager	refrigerator
smog	fidget	stagger	scrooge	manage
peg	lodger	trigger	sage	figure
slug	smudge	soggy		
	badger	slugger		
		beggar		

Using large word cards and a pocket chart, Elise demonstrated the sort, thinking aloud as she placed the individual words and gradually having the students make decisions about word placements. When the sort was complete, Elise encouraged her students to offer other words to add to the categories. The words they contributed included *fudge* and *gadget*, *dragging* and *mugging*, *stage* and *huge*, and *package* and *cigarettes*. The exception words led to an extensive discussion of how and why they are exceptions. In particular, where to place *tiger* raised questions about how the following vowel influences whether a single *g* is pronounced soft (followed by *i* or *e*) or hard (followed by *a*, *o*, or *u*). While not all the issues were resolved—these are quite complex relationships, after all—Elise's students seemed to have a better understanding of the related patterns. On the following days, students hunted for additional examples in their own reading and writing and came up with more interesting examples and exceptions, including: *ledger*, *nudged*, *maggots*, *noggin*, *clogged*, *vegetables*, and *obliged*. Each day, Elise and the group reviewed their findings and added them to the Word Wall they had constructed for the sort, deciding together on each word's appropriate placement. From the original list and the words added on the second day, Elise selected a set of 15 words for the final test. She also added three that the group had not seen but which fit the patterns. Students were encouraged to select up to seven additional words for themselves. Over the next few days, students studied their words through practice tests and/or games (see pp. 129–130). On the final day of the cycle, Elise tested the students on the group words, and student partners tested each other on their individual words. Students self-corrected their lists and handed them in. All members of the group scored at least 75% on the post-test, with many students scoring 90% or greater. Most errors were on other parts of the words (e.g., unaccented vowels). The *dg* and *gg* combinations were almost always spelled correctly. Elise was quite pleased with these results and planned to follow up with additional *g* sorts, working in hard and soft *g* words with *le*, *al*, *el*, *il*, and *ile* endings (e.g., *struggle*, *bugle*, *angel*).

Variations and Extensions: What we have just described is the basic framework for the DSTA. Of course, there are many ways that you can incorporate other aspects of word study into the DSTA lesson format. For example, we often employ a classroom Word Wall in which the week's words (as well as the previous week's words) are put on display for immediate access and practice. And certainly, the weekly words can always be sent home for more traditional practice and word games.

The Final Word: You—or you and your students together—can evaluate student progress and decide whether to move on to a new lesson or whether a review of the concepts and further practice is appropriate. Students might also add learned words to a word journal that can be used as a resource for future activities and as an overall record of spelling achievements.

As with many of the word study activities described in this book, the DSTA is not meant as a one-time lesson. The DSTA needs to be an ongoing, regular part of the reading/language arts curriculum. When it is done on a regular basis, students develop an awareness of spelling patterns and can use this knowledge to tackle (or hypothesize about) the spelling and pronunciation of new words they encounter.

Sort, Search, and Discover

What: Spelling scholars Mary Jo Fresch and Aileen Wheaton (2002) developed the Sort, Search, and Discover (SSD) procedure as "a spelling instruction strategy that assesses students' current knowledge and individualizes the study of words with common spelling patterns or rules" (p. 20). SSD is a multiday plan for spelling instruction that blends teacher direction and guidance, active learning techniques, and student decision-making

Why: Teachers and students often need set, known instructional routines to guide their study of words—SSD is a proven routine that students and teachers find engaging and beneficial.

Who: All students engaged in focused word study instruction can benefit from using SSD. Students need a working sight vocabulary and some knowledge of spelling patterns to get started.

When and Where: SSD functions as a replacement for and an improvement on the more traditional five-day spelling lesson format, so plan on 20–30 minutes a day for five days during your language arts block.

How: Sort, Search, and Discover usually follows a five-day instructional cycle that begins on Tuesday to provide weekend time for studying. Fresch and Wheaton suggest the following plan:

> *Day 1:* Select a set of words guided by your understanding of spelling development, results from a developmental spelling inventory, and your

observations and analysis of student written work. Select words below, at, and above grade level that fit the patterns you've decided your students need to study. Students take and self-correct a spelling test that uses about half the words. With your guidance, each student then selects a set of words by replacing the words they spelled correctly with words from the other half of the list. Students who are highly successful on the list can choose their own words, as long as they follow the patterns for the lesson. Next, students copy their words into three lists, one to post at home, one to attach to writing folders, and one to cut up for sorting.

Day 2: Students cut words from one list into word cards and sort them alone or with a buddy to discover the spelling patterns. You might move among them, guiding those who need your support. At first, students listen and sort by sound (for example, short vowel sounds vs. long vowels vs. *r*-controlled vowels.). Next, they study the words in each group to determine which letter combinations go with each sound pattern. Then they write their own "rules" or generalizations that explain the relationships they've discovered.

At this point, call the class together to discuss their findings. Using a pocket chart and word cards, you and your students cooperatively sort all the words into the appropriate categories. Talking through your decision-making provides a model that students can incorporate into their own thinking. Next, gather student insights and conclusions onto a generalizations chart that remains available for future reference and review.

Finally, students begin their word hunts. They do this by checking a variety of reading materials for more words that fit the patterns, both for a set amount of time (e.g., 20 minutes) and throughout the day, across the curriculum.

Day 3: Students come together to discuss the findings from their word hunts and to build an all-inclusive class list that is kept visible on a chart and stand. Next, students create written texts using the words from their individual lists. These writings often link to language arts instruction and can involve a variety of genres. They may be peer-edited and are often used in writing conferences soon afterward. Be sure to check for correct usage and spelling, since these writings will be used for the peer testing at the end of the word study cycle.

Day 4: This day is typically open-ended and flexible. Students might play word games, check word origins and histories, continue with their writings, etc. This time also provides an opportunity for you to meet with small groups or individuals.

Day 5: As a final activity, students buddy up to post-test each other using the writing activity from Day 3 as the context for presenting the words. Students read each other's writings out loud. As the reader finishes a sentence with the author's spelling word in it, the author writes it down on a list. Words can be highlighted or underlined to make the testing easier. As you circulate, you can check on correct spellings and note students scoring below 80%, who will need further review.

Variations and Extensions: Sorting words and writing a passage from a given set of words can be challenging for many students. When first introducing SSD to students, do extensive modeling to show them how it is done. Before asking students to do these activities on their own, perform sorts and write stories on your whiteboard while they watch you. Be sure to think aloud through the process of your sorting and writing so that your thinking and problem-solving become apparent to them.

Fresch and Wheaton (2002) include specific suggestions for modifying procedures for work with inclusion students. These include the following: choosing a greater variety of words for the list, providing closer guidance and more explicit modeling during word sorting, pairing inclusion students with a variety of other students or small groups to support Word Hunting, using audio recordings and/or dictation for writing in context, providing peer support during class games and activities, and providing peer or aide support when the inclusion child is required to read his or her buddy's writing.

The Final Word: Mary Jo Fresch (personal communication, November 17, 2009) has provided some observations on the impact on student learning of using the SSD framework:

> After following the SSD framework for several weeks, the students are able to independently direct selecting their words for the week. We also noticed that many of the students were beginning to see and hear the pattern during the pretest. Since we never say "this week our pattern is . . .," we encourage them to wait until the sorting day to share their discoveries about the words. Also, many of the students started bringing in words that fit the pattern that they found in books they were reading at home. During the word hunt day, we ask them to contribute those as well as any others they find that day. For the word hunts, we often use science glossaries or other content books to make the point that these patterns are everywhere and that we are learning to spell to write across the curriculum. After a while, the students spontaneously will discover that words we are discussing in other areas, such as in content vocabulary, are 'just like our spelling words this week.' Once they begin to notice these patterns in other places, we have an indication that we have raised their word awareness. This seems to carry over, then, to their independent writing.

strategy

Making Words

What: Do you recall an elementary school activity in which the teacher put a word on the chalkboard and asked all the students to try to list, on their own, as many words as possible from the letters in that given word? I think most of us remember doing something like this as students and probably enjoying the activity. It was fun. And it was also a way to learn how words work. Good students enjoyed this activity, but struggling readers and spellers were frustrated with having to think of words from a given set of letters without help.

Pat and Jim Cunningham (1992) adapted this age-old anagram activity for use with struggling readers and spellers and called it Making Words (MW). In MW, students work with a limited number of letters to build words under the guidance of the teacher. The guidance that the teacher provides to students in the activity makes it something that struggling readers can benefit from. And, of course, the enjoyment of making words in this way makes the activity feel like a game.

Why: Constructivist learning suggests that we learn by making things. Making Words is a constructivist word learning activity that challenges students to discover how words work by immersing them in arranging and rearranging a limited set of letters to build words.

Who: We like Making Words for younger students—grades K–2. The physical movement involved in rearranging letter tiles allows younger children to quickly test their hypotheses about how words are spelled and sounded. Because in any lesson students work with words that range from easy to spell to more difficult, the activity can be used with children of different reading and spelling levels.

When and Where: Making Words can be done as a small- or large-group activity. It works best within the word study portion of the reading curriculum; however, it can also be used as a transition or introductory activity in another part of the curriculum.

How: You will need to do some preparation for a Making Words lesson. Begin by determining a key word, the letters of which will be used to make words. The key word can be one that reflects a holiday or time of year, a current event, or something students may be studying in reading/language arts or another subject area. From this key word, determine in advance the words that can be made from its letters. The Wordsmith website will do this for you in a matter of seconds http://www.wordsmith.org/anagram/advanced.html (Click "Yes" to the question "Show Candidate Word List Only.")

From the letters in the word *Sylvester* (a lesson done after reading *Sylvester and the Magic Pebble*), Wordsmith generated the following words of three letters or more:

restyles	elves	steel	ever
svelter	sleet	tyre	lets
restyle	trees	seer	trey
tersely	terse	very	stye
esters	styes	ryes	lees
resets	every	eels	eyes
sleety	lever	revs	leer
vestry	revel	tees	yes
svelte	steer	sets	tee
vessel	rests	rest	vet
steels	sever	vest	yet
verses	style	sees	res
slyest	verse	less	eye
revels	tress	vets	ere
steers	elver	else	set
serest	vests	tree	sty
sleets	ester	eery	eve
levers	yeses	rely	lye
severs	treys	sere	rev
steely	leery	reel	try
elvers	tyres	eves	rye
styles	lyres	lest	lee
serves	reset	lyre	let
selves	serve	lyes	sly
lesser	seers	veer	see
veers	reels	levy	eel
slyer	leers	erst	

Essential Strategies for Word Study | **Part I: Examining Word Structure**

From this list, choose the words you want to use in your lesson. This usually ranges from 6–15 words. Put the words in order, generally from the shortest or easiest to the longest or the hardest. The final word in the lesson should be the word that contains all the letters. (In the case above, *Sylvester* would be the final word.) Working with second graders, Mr. Hertzel chose these words for this lesson:

see, set, let, tee, tree, reel, steel, sleet, rest, vest, very, ever, Sylvester

Next, cut out for each student (or have students cut out) nine squares from a sheet of paper or hard stock and write one letter from the key word on each square. Vowels and consonants can be distinguished in some way (e.g., color of the letter or the paper on which the letters are written). Although this may seem a tedious task, teachers have found ingenious ways to make it quick and simple. Then present each student with the nine letters. You should have a large version of the letters and a pocket chart so that you can do the lesson with your students and allow them to watch you manipulate your letters. The lesson is now ready to begin.

In the lesson, you simply guide your students to make the words you had planned by arranging and rearranging the nine letters. As you and your students make the words, point out to them salient features of the words—for example, vowel and consonant sounds, vowel digraphs (*ee*), consonant blends (*st*), *r*-controlled vowels (*er*), number of syllables, and, of course, the meaning of each word. Help students see how often one word is built from previous words, with only a small manipulation required.

The final word in each lesson is always the key (also called the magic, secret, or challenge) word. It is the word that uses all the letters. For this last word, no clues are given initially. Students need to try to figure it out on their own. Knowing that the word is related to a current event, a previously read book, or an upcoming holiday, students are usually able to figure out this final word. They take great delight in being able to outfox their teacher. If students are unable to come up with the last word, you can give them the first, second letters and so on, or provide them with other clues that will allow them to be successful.

You can expand the lesson in several ways. First, you can find a letter pattern or two that you explored in the lesson and have students write new words using the pattern but now using all the letters of the alphabet (*A–Z*). For example, in the *Sylvester* lesson you could have students make these additional words:

-et: bet, get, jet, met, net, pet, wet, letter, wetter, settle, kettle

and

-est: test, west, crest, best, guest, Chester, pester, festival

Once all your words are made, students can then sort them in various ways—by letter and sound pattern, number of syllables, number of letters, grammatical category, etc. Certain interesting words can also be added to the Word Wall for further practice and use.

Variations and Extensions: There are all kinds of ways to extend and vary Making Words. Teachers who may not see themselves as reading teachers can easily make use of MW. A math, social studies, art, or music teacher or the school librarian can create his or her own MW lessons—the key word would simply be one that comes from something that students have recently studied (or will be studying). And parents can easily learn to develop and use this activity at home with their children.

Even students themselves can learn to do MW, once they know the routine. Simply give a student the key word. That student's task is to determine words that can be made from the letters of the key word, put them in the order of presentation, and think of clues to share with classmates when he or she actually teaches the lesson to a group. Being teachers, we have all learned the power of teaching others. When we teach others, we have to learn something at a deeper level. When we have students act as teachers of their classmates (MW is a natural for this), they will have to learn the words they are going to teach at a much deeper level than if they were on the receiving end of the instruction.

The Final Word: Making Words works! It is a regular and productive part of our own work with struggling readers. We try to do an MW lesson at least twice a week. Pat Cunningham and her colleagues (Cunningham, et al., 1998; 2006) have done classroom-based research with elementary students in which MW is a central element. Students in classrooms where MW is featured make remarkable progress in phonics, spelling, and reading. Reported progress is well above what would normally be expected, given the demographics of the schools and the progress previously made by students!

strategy

Making and Writing Words

What: Most good educational methods are variants or innovations of methods that have been previously described. As we suggested earlier, Pat and Jim Cunningham's Making Words is a variation of the old anagram game that teachers have been doing for years with children. We developed Making and Writing Words (MWW) (Rasinski, 1999a, 1999b) as a variation on Making Words. The intent of MWW was for older students to have an opportunity to actually write the words they are making.

Why: As we mentioned in the previous chapter, Making Words is a constructivist activity in which students actually make words under the guidance of a teacher. Writing the words, as well as seeing, saying, spelling, and talking about them, makes learning the words a multisensory experience (Birsh, 2005). The inclusion of additional senses makes it easier for struggling readers and spellers to learn new words.

Who: Making and Writing Words can be used at any grade level, but we like using MWW after students have had some experience with Making Words. It seems particularly well suited for students in grades 3 and above. As with Making Words, because students work with words that range from easy to more challenging in any lesson, MWW can be used with children at different reading and spelling levels.

When and Where: Making and Writing Words can be done as a small- or large-group activity. It works best within the word study portion of the reading curriculum, but it can also be used as a transition or introductory activity in another part of the curriculum.

How: The preparation for Making and Writing Words is the same as for Making Words. Using the www.wordsmith.org/anagram/advanced.html website, we found the following words of three or more letters that could be made from *independence*. (Tim recently did this lesson with some fourth- and fifth-grade struggling readers the day before the Fourth of July.)

dependence	niece	pend
deepened	diced	cede
decide	dined	inn
denied	ceded	ice
pieced	need	din
depend	nine	nip
indeed	epic	die
pinned	dice	did
deepen	pine	dip
penned	iced	pic
pended	deed	nee
dinned	nice	pin
needed	died	end
pined	épée	den
deice	peen	pee
piece	pied	pie
ended	deep	pen
pence	dine	

Essential Strategies for Word Study | **Part I: Examining Word Structure**

From this list, choose 10–15 words you will want to use with your students. Put the words in order, generally from the shortest or easiest to the longest or the hardest. The final word in the lesson will be *independence*.

Here are the words Tim chose for his lesson: *pie, die, dine, dice, nice, niece, need, deed, indeed, depend, decide, denied, independence*. (Tim chose 13 words for this lesson in honor of the 13 states that declared their independence in 1776!)

Making and Writing Words differs from Making Words in the way that the lesson is implemented. Instead of using letter tiles to make the words, the students write the letters and words in the appropriate boxes on the MWW response form (see below for thumbnails of forms for primary grades and for grade 2+; for reproducible forms, see Appendix, pp. 143–144). As with MW, you guide your students to write the words you had planned for your lesson, beginning with *pie* and ending with the key word *independence*. As you and your students make the words, point out to them (and have them mark on their response sheets) salient features of the words (e.g., digraphs, blends, silent letters, phonics irregularities, etc.). The final word in each lesson is always the key (or the magic, secret, or challenge) word.

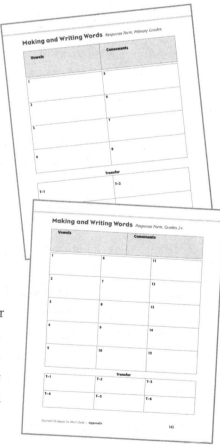

As with MW, you can expand the lesson in several ways. First, you can find a letter pattern or two that you explored in the lesson and have students write new words using the pattern, but now using all the letters of the alphabet. With older students, you can use letter patterns, such as word families and affixes; you can also use derivational patterns from Latin and Greek. In the *independence* lesson, we expanded on the Latin root *pend* (which means to weigh, hang, or attach), talked about how the words we already made, *depend* and *independence*, have a meaning that is connected to *hang*, and made the following words:

> *pend: pending, append, appendix, appendage, pendant,*
> *pendulum, suspend, suspenders, suspension*

Once all your words are made, students can then sort them in various ways—by letter and sound pattern, number of syllables, grammatical category, meaning, etc. Particularly interesting words can also be added to the Word Wall for further practice and use.

Variations and Extensions: The same variations and extensions that we mentioned in Making Words can be applied to Making and Writing Words. Instead of using vowels and consonants as your building blocks, you can also use letter patterns, such as word families, affixes, and derivational word roots, along with individual letters as your building blocks. You can find more on this in an article Tim wrote for Reading Online at http://readingonline.org/articles/art_index. asp?HREF=rasinski/index.html (Rasinski, 1999b).

Some teachers combine Making Words with MWW. Students manipulate letter tiles in making their words. Once the correct spelling is established, students write each word in the appropriate box of the MWW response sheet.

The Final Word: Making and Writing Words is the natural expansion of Making Words. Using the response sheet rather than letter tiles does take away a bit of the logistical challenge for some teachers and students. And writing the words does help make the words more permanently established in the student's memory. Perhaps the thing we like most of all about MWW (and Making Words as well) is that the activity feels like a game to most students. Struggling readers and spellers don't often get to play the games in school because the games are only played when the work is done, and struggling readers rarely get their work done in time. All students can play MWW; more important, it develops readers, spellers, and writers at the same time!

Word Sorts

Why: Word Sorting is an activity in which words are written on cards so they can be quickly and easily organized into different categories. You can use Word Sorts in manipulative activities in which students organize words on cards into columns according to specific categories. Students decide where to place each word, depending on shared and contrasting features of the words to be sorted.

Why: Word Sorts can help students more carefully examine, understand, and internalize the features of words and/or the concepts they represent. They help students improve their word identification and spelling skills and to examine important concepts in subject areas.

Who: Word Sorts have been used across grade levels and subject areas, though they were first developed to support student word learning for reading and spelling. The procedures are basically the same, but the complexity of patterns and/or ideas changes with student knowledge and skills. While you can use Word Sorts with students of all ability levels, they are especially powerful for helping struggling readers and spellers who do not easily see and use word patterns.

When and Where: You can use Word Sorts to follow up after the introductory discussion about important word features or patterns. They are often done first in a large group, then as small-group and individual activities. For word study, you might select the patterns to be studied based on the results of qualitative spelling assessments, word identification tests, or on the content of basal reading or spelling lessons.

How: Here is a set of steps for using Word Sorts in individual or paired word study. You can easily modify them for small-group, teacher-led sorting:

- Select patterns for study based on what students are "using but confusing." They typically know high-frequency and/or other familiar words that follow these patterns but are unsure how to use the patterns to figure out less familiar words.

- You or an aide or volunteer neatly write individual words with the patterns or features on blank index cards or strips that can be cut into cards.

- Select a key word or pattern to head each column. Use a "question mark" card/column for exceptions. Underlining the letter combinations that students are meant to attend to helps them keep their focus.

- Gather the remaining cards into a stack with the words facedown.

- You (or an aide or a student's classmate) select a card and read it, then use the word in a sentence and read it again without showing the word to the student.

- The student chooses the column where he or she thinks the word fits.

- You (or an aide or a student's classmate) show the student the word card.

- The student has the opportunity to compare the word on the card with the key words and the words already in the columns. The student then decides whether to add the word to the column he or she originally chose or to put it somewhere else.

Variations and Extensions: Spelling or Orthographic Sorts focus on the relationship between pronunciation or meaning and spelling patterns (e.g., short vowel vs. long vowel spellings in single-syllable words). **Concept Sorts** are based on word meanings irrespective of individual spellings (e.g., happy vs. sad words). When you select the categories for sorting, you are organizing **Closed Sorts**. If students are given a set of words and are free to choose their own categories, they are doing **Open Sorts**. In **Visual Sorts,** students look at the words as they sort them, so they can use a combination of visual information and word pronunciation as they make their decisions. **Blind Sorts** are more demanding than Visual Sorts because students choose where to place the words *before* seeing them. A teacher or partner reads the word to the sorter without showing it to her or him. Thus the sorters are "blind" to how the words look. They must use word pronunciations and/or meanings as clues to visual patterns, or use their mental images of the words to decide what patterns they follow, and thus where to place the words. **Speed Sorts** are variations of Visual Sorts in which students place the words in the correct columns accurately and as fast as they can. To this end, Speed Sorts help students develop greater automaticity with words and patterns. **Writing to the Sort** is a more challenging extension of Blind Sorting. Instead of placing cards in the appropriate columns, students are required to produce a full and accurate spelling for each of the words. But this activity is more supportive than a simple spelling test because students have the sorting categories in columns with key words on the paper in front of them to help them decide how words with those patterns should be spelled.

When focusing on a particular aspect of word learning, you would normally choose words for sorting. However, any group of words can be sorted in one way or another. That said, word sorting can be done with nearly any other activity described in this book. For example, the words used in Word Ladders, Making Words, Making and Writing Words, Synonym/Antonym Word Ladders, and words from Word Harvests can easily be sorted in various ways—into categories that you define as well as creative categories that students themselves determine.

Several variations of word sorts can be used together to reinforce learning, usually moving from teacher-guided to independent and from less demanding to more demanding (e.g., Visual to Blind to Writing to the Sort).

The Final Word: Teachers we have worked with in the classroom and clinic often attest to the power and effectiveness of Word Sorting, once they have begun to use this activity regularly with their students. Here is a sample of some of the observations they have shared with us:

◆   "Sorting gives me a window into how my students think about
       words and what they notice about them."

- "Small-group/buddy sorting leads to interesting conversations—students begin to take on the language of words and own the patterns."

- "My students are eager to work with their words this way. They often work on sorting without having to be told and challenge each other to discover the categories they've worked out."

- "Having words on cards is really powerful because moving words next to each other gives my students a direct comparison and a way to locate the patterns across words, something my struggling readers and writers have a lot of difficulty doing."

- "I now realize that when I talked about word structure I would often use terms (vowel, consonants, vowel patterns, silent-*e*) my struggling readers had heard but didn't really understand. Through sorting they have begun to own these terms, for the first time understanding what they mean and how to apply them."

- "Doing two things together—e.g., looking *and* listening—is sometimes difficult for struggling readers. Sorting helps them to develop that skill."

- "The first time I took the same set of words and sorted them two different ways, my students thought it was magic! They had never conceived that you could look at the same words so many different ways. Sorting helps them step back and get the big picture about how words work."

Sorting or categorizing is a task that scientists perform to better understand and make sense of their fields of study. Botanists study and categorize plants, zoologists study and categorize animals, astronomers study and categorize celestial objects. When we place students in the position of categorizing or sorting words, we are giving them a tool for studying and making discoveries about the spelling, meaning, and structure of words.

Word Families and Decodable Texts (Word Family Poems)

What: One of the most productive approaches to teaching phonics is through word families (what others have called phonograms or rimes). A word family is a combination of letters that have a very consistent sound to them. Specifically, a word family is the part of a syllable that begins with the vowel and contains any consonants that come after the vowel that are also within the same syllable. A decodable text is simply a short passage that contains many examples of whatever phonics element you are teaching.

Why: The consistency and frequency of word families make them worth teaching. Using word families (and other word patterns) to decode words is an extremely efficient approach to phonics; rather than decoding words one letter at a time, students decode words using the two, three, or four letters in a word family as a single unit. Moreover, word families are ubiquitous in English words. According to Edward Fry (1998), knowledge of the 38 most common word families (see below) can help students read and spell 654 one-syllable words simply by adding a beginning consonant, consonant blend, or consonant digraph. The number of multisyllabic words that contain these word families goes into the tens of thousands!

Who: Word family instruction is most often aimed at students in grades K–2. However, for students who struggle in phonics or word decoding, regardless of grade level, instruction in word families and other word patterns is very appropriate.

When and Where: For primary-grade students, word family instruction should occur during the daily time allotted for word study. Reading of decodable texts can occur at any time of the day. In the Kent State University reading clinics, students read decodable texts at the beginning and end of each day.

How: There are many ways to teach word families. A simple multiday approach that we find very productive follows these steps.

Day 1: Introduce a word family to students and make a list of all the words that contain that word family; be sure to include some multisyllabic words in your list. Practice these words with students several times, read them in different orders, and have students write the words in their own personal word journals. For example, if you studied the –*at* word family, the following words could be listed for students to read:

> *-at: cat, fat, bat, rat, brat, flat, mat, hat, chat, that, battle, cattle, rattle, bobcat, habitat*

Day 2: Review the words from Day 1. Then introduce a second word family, going through the same routine as in Day 1. Here's an example using the –*et* word family:

> *-et: bet, set, get, jet, let, met, net, pet, wet, settle, metal, petals, jacket*

Day 3: Review both lists of words from Days 1 and 2, then create a third list of words that is a combination of words from both days. The list might look like this:

> *bat, bet, jet, wet, battle, jacket, net, flat, chat, settle, petals, cattle, bobcat, pet*

Review and practice these words several times over Day 3. The reason for combining the list is that if a list of words contains only one word family, the list becomes very predictable and students get to the point where they do not have to look at a word closely in order to read it correctly. (Since they know that all the words in the Day 1 list contain the sound /at/, students get to the point where they only have to look at the first letter to decode most of the words.) Combining the words from two or more lists means that students have to look more closely at the words because they cannot be so certain about the sounds represented by the word families. The words presented throughout these three days can also be used in various games (e.g., WORDO) or other word study activities (e.g., Word Ladders).

Day 4: After reviewing the Day 3 list one more time, students read decodable texts chorally, in pairs, and on their own. Instead of the decodable texts that many teachers and students have come to dread (e.g., "Dan the man had a tan"), we recommend the use of rhyming poetry as a type of decodable text that students will find engaging and enjoyable to read and reread. Rhyming poetry by its very nature contains words with word families (words in a word family rhyme). At this point, then, a poem such as the following would be great for students to read

> Jack Sprat could eat no fat
> His wife could eat no lean
> And so between the two of them
> They licked the platter clean!

And if you can't find a poem, you can write your own for your students. Here's one Tim wrote that features the *–et* word family.

> Diddle diddle dumpling Betty and Bret
> Would always worry and would always fret.
> They fretted about their children and they fretted about their pet.
> Diddle diddle dumpling Betty and Bret.

The rhythm, rhyme, and brevity of poems for children make them ideal for reading and rereading. Not only will students be practicing the targeted word families, they will also be exposed to other words that through repeated exposure and Harvesting Words (see pp. 125–127) will become part of students' reading vocabulary as well.

Variations and Extensions: We would love to see every school that teaches word families have a collection of poems organized around different word families. If you are a reading coach or principal, think of developing such a repository. Simply take an empty file drawer and get about 200 file folders. Label each file folder with a word family that is part of your curriculum. Then, any time there is a faculty meeting, ask teachers and other staff members to come with a rhyming poem—one they find or one they write themselves. Before long, your school will have a wonderful and growing compendium of poems that teachers and students can use to develop their phonics skills and reading proficiency (and have fun at the same time). If you are a classroom teacher reading this, you can develop your own classroom compendium of poems in the same way. Grade-level teachers can also work on their own specialized group of word families.

If Tim can write his own poem, then certainly children can, too. Once students have seen their teacher share poems that he or she has written, they can create their own without much difficulty. Certainly, they will have all the rhyming words in front of them. Can you imagine students writing their own version of "Jack Sprat," using words that belong to the –*et* word family?

> Chet Spret's pet is always wet
> While Chet is never dry
> And between the two of them
> His mom says, "My oh my!"

The Final Word: Tim and Jerry are known for their work in reading fluency. Reading fluency, a critical competency in reading, is best taught through repeated guided oral reading. The decodable poems that we advocate here are ideal not only for word family instruction but also to develop fluency. The repeated reading of decodable poems can be a huge aid in helping young students develop fluency and expressiveness in their reading.

The Most Common Word Families (Phonograms)

By adding a beginning letter or letters to these word families, students can spell and read 654 one-syllable words!

-ab	-ay	-ine	-ow (how, chow)
-ack	-ed	-ink	-ow (low, throw)
-ag	-eed	-in	-out
-ail	-ell	-ing	-unk
-ain	-est	-ip	-y
-am	-ew	-ob	-uck
-an	-ill	-op	-ug
-ank	-ick	-ock	-um
-ap	-ight	-ore	
-at	-im	-ot	

strategy

Derivational Word Webs

What: Many words are related to one another in that they share word parts that have similar meanings across words. A Derivational Word Web is a graphic organizer that helps students see the relationships among words that share these parts, their spellings, and their meanings.

Why: Research indicates that many English words, particularly academic words and words learned beyond the primary grades, are built by combining prefixes, roots, and/or suffixes. Students who recognize word parts and understand how they are put together can use this knowledge as an aid to determining word meanings and making connections between words that may not sound the same but share the same spelling patterns and have similar meanings. Often, a significant number of words can be generated from a single root.

Who: Derivational Word Webbing is an appropriate activity for students in the later stages of word knowledge, as described in Ehri's Consolidated Alphabetic and Automatic phases (Ehri & McCormick, 2004) or the developmental spelling stages of late Syllable Juncture and Derivational Constancy (e.g., Scharer & Zutell, 2003). (See pp. 16–17). This stage would typically cover third grade and beyond.

When and Where: You can use webbing as a part of the word study curriculum for spelling and meaning vocabulary, in developing word analysis skills, as a tool for studying Latin, Greek, and other roots, and as a vocabulary follow-up to reading activities in which such words are encountered.

How: Derivational Word Webs begin with a box in the center of a page or chart where you write the root and its main variations along with a brief definition (see p. 49). From the center, lines or "spokes" are drawn to boxes at the edges of the chart or page. It's often helpful to write a category label or suffix at the top of each box to give students direction as to what words should go inside. Alternatively, some boxes might be left unlabeled so that students can add their own categories or prefixes. You might also provide examples in the boxes or elicit examples from the students during discussion. Students work as a class, in small groups, or individually to brainstorm words to fit the different categories or boxes. As students discuss their contributions, they also provide brief definitions of their words. When appropriate, you can encourage them to connect their definitions of the whole word to the meanings of the parts.

Variations and Extensions: Similar word-building activities can be done in simple rows and columns, although they are less visually appealing. You can also decide how much information and how many examples to provide. The activity can also be done as a game in which students take turns and gain points for each new word and its definition. Other players may challenge words and gain points for corrections, while players who are caught offering incorrect responses lose points. In another variation, students gain points for making up new plausible words whose meanings are consistent with the meanings of their various parts.

The Final Word: After students have successfully participated in completing several webs, you can follow up with a more varied activity in which you give students sets of prefixes, roots, and suffixes and ask them to construct as many different words as they can. Again, this can be done in a game format.

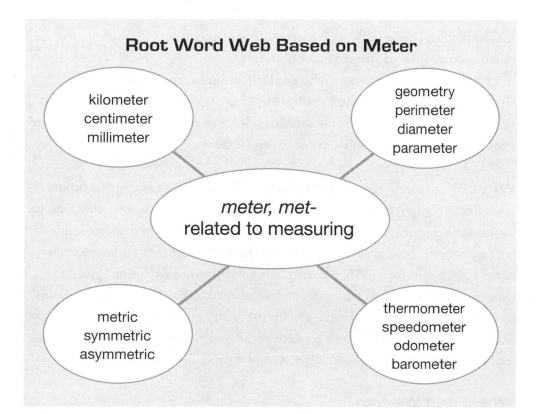

Root Word Web Based on Meter

kilometer
centimeter
millimeter

geometry
perimeter
diameter
parameter

meter, met-
related to measuring

metric
symmetric
asymmetric

thermometer
speedometer
odometer
barometer

"Be the Bard"—Student Word Inventions

What: Have you ever thought about how words come to be? How are words actually invented? In his book *Frindle*, Andrew Clements does a wonderful job of telling the story of how a young wordsmith by the name of Nick invented a new word. Perhaps the greatest wordsmith of all time was William Shakespeare. Literary scholars suggest that he added approximately 2,000 words to written English through his own writing. Words such as *jaded, eyeball, bedroom, skim milk, premeditated, blood-stained, countless, courtship*, and *birthplace* are just a few of the many words credited to the Bard. Did you notice that most of the words and terms are compounds of existing words or word parts? Shakespeare simply combined existing words or word parts to make new words.

We think Shakespeare is a pretty good fellow for students to emulate. If Shakespeare can make new words, why can't students? That is what Be the Bard is all about—inviting students to use their knowledge of existing words, concepts, and word parts to create new words, concepts, and ideas.

Why: We are strong advocates of constructivist learning—learning that occurs when one is engaged in the act of making something. In this case, the act of making words will help students solidify their understanding not only of the words they are creating but, more important, the words and word parts they use to make their new words. Be the Bard (BTB) is particularly valuable when exploring Latin and Greek roots or derivations with students. Many words in English are derived from Latin and Greek (and other languages, for that matter). When students use Latin and Greek roots to create new words, they are forced to dig deep into the meaning of the root itself and they will begin to take notice of the root in other English words.

When and Where: BTB is a fun, creative activity that fits well as an extension to the study of morphology in English, in particular Latin and Greek roots. It can also be a center activity that students can go to whenever they feel that creative urge.

How: BTB requires students to have a foundation of Latin and Greek roots and affixes. However, students can also use other English words, prefixes, and suffixes that are not necessarily derived from Latin and Greek. Once students develop a corpus of roots and affixes, simply ask them to begin combining the word parts and develop a definition that accurately defines the newly invented word. It is very helpful if you can share with students examples of words that you have invented yourself or that were invented by students in previous years.

Once students see what you mean by BTB, they can engage in making one, two, or more words. Have them share the oral and written form of their new words with their classmates and challenge them to determine the meaning of the word and use it in a real-life context. Developing and sharing the words should take approximately 20 minutes. The newly minted words can then be placed on display for others to see, use, and define. By inviting students to "be the Bard" once a week during a word study session, you will not only develop and deepen students' knowledge of these roots that are so essential to academic learning, you will also help them take great delight in words and in the creative use and employment of words. Don't be surprised to see your students (and yourself) using the invented words throughout the year. When that happens, you know you have them hooked on words.

In the Kent State University reading clinic a few years ago, a fourth grader walked into class with a riddle he had developed after playing BTB in class. He said, "Hey guys, I just invented a new word—*autophile*! If you are an autophile, what would you most likely have in your pocket or purse—a wad of money, a set of car keys, or a mirror?" All the students responded immediately with "Car keys! An autophile is someone who loves autos." Our young wordsmith responded, "Wrong! The correct answer is *mirror*. An autophile is a person who is in love with himself or herself. This person would often be found looking at himself or herself in a mirror." We thought this was quite a clever riddle from a student who was quickly becoming a *lexophile*! The exchange in class led to an interesting discussion of why automobiles have been given this name, which led naturally to thinking about how the early observers of cars, or horseless carriages, were struck by the thought that these vehicles seemed to move by themselves, on their own, without any visible form of propulsion.

Here are some other words invented by upper elementary and middle school students (see below for definitions):

matermand, teleterra, pentopolis, aquatract

Variations and Extensions: BTB can be expanded to include words and word parts that do not have a Latin or Greek root.

The Final Word: Traditionally, students have been asked to learn words by copying and memorizing words in a dictionary, even though the dictionary definitions are often of little help in understanding what the words actually mean. In BTB, students create words using common English word roots and affixes. Who do you think will have a better understanding of words—the student who is passively involved in searching a dictionary or the student who is actively involved in creating meaning? The answer for us is clear. We hope it is for you as well. *Carpe verba*!

Definitions of Words Invented by Students

matermand: A mother's order or command

teleterra: A distant land

pentopolis: A group of five cities (New York City, which consists of five boroughs, may be considered a pentopolis.)

aquatract: A person who is pulled toward or attracted to water; one who lives near an ocean, lake, or other body of water—another word, perhaps, for a hydrophiliac!

Word Origins Notebook

What: A Word Origins Notebook is a simple technique for gathering and organizing interesting and valuable information about vocabulary words within and across subject areas.

Why: Word Origins Notebooks spark student curiosity about where words come from and how they are made. They also help to make the words and their meanings easier to remember.

Who: Word Origins Notebooks are most appropriate and useful for students in upper elementary grades and beyond. While you may use them for your specific subject area, they are especially effective when they are initiated by a team of teachers working across the curriculum. In such situations, the literacy teacher will often take the lead in getting the notebooks started, monitoring their use, and providing time for students to share their entries.

When and Where: After an initial explanation and discussion, building a notebook is usually an independent, ongoing activity, except that the teacher plans a regular daily or weekly time for sharing and reflection.

How: You begin with a lesson explaining the many ways words have become part of our language and illustrating your points with many examples. Sources of words we use include: 1) old words from English's Anglo-Saxon origins (*child*, *sun*); 2) words built from Latin, Greek, Anglo-Saxon, and French prefixes, roots, and suffixes (*inscribe, telephone, unhappy, journal*); 3) words adopted or adapted from other languages (*tortilla, vanilla*); 4) words from the proper names of people or products (eponyms) or places (toponyms), such as *sandwich*, *Kleenex*, and *manila*; 5) short words made from longer ones (*taxi* and *cab* from *taxicab*); 6) words made from the beginning letters of phrases or complex names (acronyms like *scuba*); or words built from the parts of two other words (portmanteau words like *brunch*). You can point out that good dictionaries and other sources provide information about a word's origin.

Word Origins Notebooks consist of pages organized into columns with at least the following headings: 1) Word, 2) What Does It Mean? 3) Where Does It Come From? 4) How Was It Made? You and your students can assemble individual sections for specific topics or a specific subject area.

In order to locate the information needed to construct such a notebook, you and your students will need several sources to locate such information, including scholarly works on the history of the English language, more popular (and readable) books on word origins, a variety of traditional and online dictionaries, and amusing/interesting books about words written for school-age children. Simply Googling "word origins" will bring up a number of useful sites. Word Safari is a site that provides links to a wide variety of word sites, including many on English word origins. It can be found at http://home.earthlink.net/~ruthpett/safari/megalist. htm. (It's wise to check any site that you use in class to ensure that its content is appropriate for children). Not all sources always agree about where a word comes from, so it can be interesting to consider different theories and evidence. We've provided a starter list for you on p. 142, Selected List of Resources: Word Origins and Expressions. A more extensive list, including children's books that play on words, can be found at http://www.timrasinski.com/?page=presentations.

Variations and Extensions: Word origins can also be used as a word-of-the-day activity. Many teachers introduce a new word or two to students each day of the school year. In addition to providing students with the meaning of the daily words, sharing with them the underlying story behind the word can deepen students' interest in words and their origins.

The Final Word: It's been said that the human mind is programmed for stories. We learn through stories. Think of what we do when we get together with friends, when we attend a movie or play, when we gather in places of worship: we tell stories, we observe stories, we hear and learn through stories. Word origins are, in essence, stories about words. By sharing interesting vignettes about words, we are developing in students a fascination for where words come from, and we may even provide insight into human history and other areas of the school curriculum.

Word Origins Map

What: English is a language that knows no boundaries—literally as well as figuratively. When speakers and writers of English encounter speakers and writers of other languages, it is not unusual for English to take on some of the words from the other language. A Word Origins Map, then, is a poster that displays the connections between words that have come into English from other languages and the locations of their origins.

Why: Studying word origins helps students see language as a living, growing system of connections within and across peoples, countries, and periods of time. Building a map provides a visual representation of student findings, illustrates the number of connections, and increases memory for vocabulary words and the concepts they represent. Such maps also create a link between history, geography, and word study instruction.

Who: Contributing to a Word Origins Map is an appropriate activity for students in the upper elementary grades and beyond who are engaged in studying word origins. Students should be familiar with using dictionaries and other sources that contain word origin information. This activity supports and extends the building of a Word Origins Notebook (see pp. 53–54).

When and Where: Finding words and researching their origins for the map is an independent activity that students can choose to do as part of word study. It can also find its way into your word study center. You might assign your students individually or in pairs to research a specific word, but more often you will want to encourage them to notice interesting words that they hear or come across in their reading. Your students can explore words and their meanings and sources, add them to their Word Origins Notebook, contribute them to the map, and discuss their findings during a daily or weekly group sharing time.

How: Begin with a large, current world map mounted to a wall or bulletin board in your class. The map should be low enough so that students can reach both individual countries and outlying edges for mounting their words. Provide students with yarn, pins, and blank cards or strips. Explain to your students that as they come across new or unusual words, they can show the connection between the word and its origin by using the pin to attach one end of the yarn to the country of origin and the other end to the card at the outer end of the map or in one of the large bodies of water. Have students write the word, country of origin, and, if known, date of entry into English on the card. On p. 142 and on the web at http://www.timrasinski. com/?page=presentations you'll find lists of word origin books and websites.

Margaret Miller, one of our former students, teaches fifth grade in an urban elementary school. She has always been fascinated by words and was inspired by class presentations and examples to encourage her own students to become "word detectives." Reading the vocabulary research also helped her realize that students who are curious about words, their meanings, and origins are more likely to develop extensive vocabularies for reading and writing and to become more critical readers and precise writers. She is determined to provide her students with the opportunity to develop and pursue this curiosity.

Maggie begins each year with an introduction to her class about their study of Word Origins, generally following the description in the "how" section on Word Origins Notebooks (pp. 53–54). Students learn that using a Word Origins Map will be an important part of that study. As one of their assignments or as part of class participation, they are expected to notice interesting and/or unusual words in their readings, to research word meanings and origins, to keep track of these words in a Word Origins Notebook, and to choose at least one word each week to share with the class.

Maggie teaches a brief lesson on the Word Origins Map. She gathers her students around a world map posted in an accessible but slightly out-of-the-way place in the classroom. She begins a discussion of what the map represents—different places on the earth, nearby or far away. She does not expect students to know the names of every geographic area or country, but they understand that they may need to work to locate a place once they learn a word's point of origin.

Maggie demonstrates using a topic familiar to her students—words related to food. Examples include *hamburger* (Germany, 1889), *frankfurter* (Germany, 1894), *ketchup* (Malaysia, 1711), *macaroni* (Italy, 1599). Maggie also demonstrates how to use geography sources to locate unfamiliar countries (e.g., Malaysia). She shows the students how to use yarn and stick-pins to connect words on cards with their place on the map, and she also records information about place and time period on the back of the card so that when she removes the cards to make space for others, they can be filed for future reference. Later, students might sort them by location or time period.

Here are some examples of words students found and mapped during one school year: *curry* (Sri Lanka, 1681), *typhoon* (from Greece, 1555 and/or China, 1588), *curfew* (France, 1320), *armada* (Spain, 1533), and *banjo* (Africa, 1764). You can see how this is a wonderful way to get students interested in how even everyday English is affected by people and places from around the world!

Word Origins Map

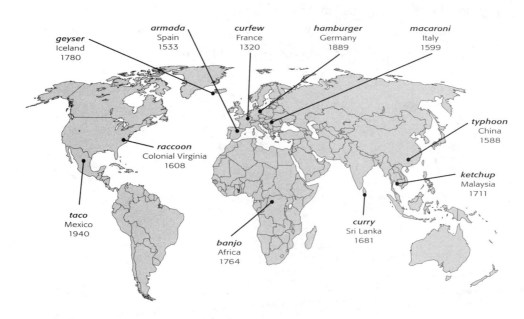

Variations and Extensions: Instead of a map, some teachers find a "river of English" metaphor to be especially powerful in illustrating how and when words have entered our language. The river serves as a timeline on which individual words can be represented as small streams, while major changes can be represented as larger tributaries. For example, the approximately 2,000 words that scholars believe Shakespeare added to written English would be represented as a small river flowing into a larger one.

Another possibility is to reverse directions and begin with a country or region of origin that has contributed words to English. Wikipedia has a page where students can look up words from other languages and trace the words to their source: http://en.wikipedia.org/wiki/Lists_of_English_words_of_international_origin.

The Final Word: During sharing time, students can provide fuller explanations of words and connections, such as a word's original meaning, current meaning, origin, and any other interesting details. Over time, students might well notice clusters of words from particular places and spelling patterns associated with words from a specific language (e.g., the *ph* in *phone* and the *rh* in *rhapsody* and other words from Greek). You may also lead them in this direction through your own questions and comments. These sorts of activities and discussions encourage students to make the connection between world history and word history!

Exploring Word Meanings

The activities in **Part II focus on discovering and exploring the connections between words and the concepts they represent. We examine words and their meanings in terms of their relationships** to other words and meanings and to the contexts in which they are used.

Theme, Context, Roots, Reference, and Review (TC3R)

What: Theme, Context, Roots, Reference, and Review (TC3R) is an organizational framework for structuring focused, conceptually based vocabulary instruction. It can be used with teacher-selected words or as the structure of a basal vocabulary program (e.g., *Word Wisdom*, Zutell, 2005).

Why: Recent research clearly shows the importance of increasing the breadth and depth of student meaning vocabularies (National Reading Panel Report, 2000). Students need more focused and direct vocabulary instruction, and you need a systematic plan for delivering that instruction. You can develop your own plan, or you may choose to draw on successful instructional frameworks that already exist. TC3R is one such framework. These instructional frameworks must make sense to students, involve a reasonable set of useful words, and develop strategies for using context, word structure, and reference sources to uncover word meanings.

Who: The TC3R model is most appropriate for and most often used with students in upper elementary and middle school grades (grades 3–8). Zutell and Scharer (2007) have developed a variation for working with primary-grade students.

When and Where: The TC3R model can be used as a regular part of literacy instruction. It can also be used by content teachers who wish to incorporate a strong vocabulary component into their subject-area instruction.

How: The steps in using TC3R include the following:

◆ **Selecting a theme and readings.** Each unit of study is organized around a conceptual theme to build strong meaning relationships among the words and with the concepts they represent. Individual teachers or teams select themes that are important parts of the curriculum or that support the curriculum. Themes may be specific (e.g., money for economics, water mammals for science) or more general (e.g., communication). Literacy teachers are more likely to choose more generic themes. You select a set of readings at the students' instructional level to cover the content of the theme. These may be from required texts, supplementary materials, or available trade books.

◆ **Selecting words.** Review the selected theme and materials to determine key vocabulary for understanding the content. Then select important but less familiar words that students will need to know. Next, review the selected vocabulary to find roots (usually at least two or three) used to form words relevant to the theme. You can expand the roots to provide additional words. (In the example below the words are taken from three roots connected to *breaking* and/or *twisting*: *-fract-, -rupt-, and -tort-*. Consider also how these might be connected to a discussion of or unit on earthquakes and volcanoes.) Then organize the materials into individual readings, each of which includes a selection of the words you intend to study. Ideally, one reading will include a number of words from the roots selected for examination.

Latin Roots and English Words
for Focus Unit: Break/Twist

Root Forms	Words
-fract-	fracture, fragment, fragile
-rupt-	erupt, rupture, interrupted, disruption
-tort-	contorted, distortion, torque

◆ **Assessing and Processing Word Meanings.** Each of the lessons based on a reading begins with a group Vocabulary Prediction

Chart (p. 72) and individual charts for the students (p. 70). Students make their best guesses as to the meaning of each word. Then they share these in a brief group discussion and enter their guesses into the group chart. Next, you choose how the selection will be read (e.g., aloud by you, silently by the students, or a combination of oral and silent reading) and then discuss the text using a Before-During-After model to enhance comprehension. Give your students direction and time to revisit the focus words in the context of the reading; they revise their predictions as they think appropriate. Again, share the results with the class or group

♦ **Working on Strategy Instruction.** Early in each lesson, teach or review at least one of three strategies to help discover word meanings: Using Context, Using Word Structure, or Using Reference Sources. You can use specific words from the lesson's list as examples. While you may highlight one strategy, encourage students to use all three in combination to come up with their final definitions and then share them. With your guidance, the group decides upon a final definition for each word.

♦ **Processing and Applying Word Meanings.** In the remainder of each lesson, students do several activities to reinforce their learning. These might include matching words with friendly definitions (Beck, McKeown, & Kucan, 2002) or everyday expressions, using the words to complete cloze passages related to the reading, deciding among possible sentences (Stahl & Nagy, 2006), or using the words in a writing assignment about the readings.

♦ **Connecting and Reviewing.** In a final lesson, all words studied in the previous lessons are used in a variety of activities that might include a large meaning-related sort, synonym and/or antonym matches, multiple-choice questions, and other test-like activities. Test-like items not only reinforce student learning but also give students familiarity, experience, and confidence with the kinds of

Essential Strategies for Word Study | **Part II: Exploring Word Meanings**

questions they are likely to find on standardized tests. Sometimes this is necessary so that students can fully demonstrate what they know and avoid being penalized by the form of the test itself.

Variations and Extensions: *Word Wisdom* (Zutell, 2005) is a carefully structured vocabulary textbook series built on this model. Each unit in *Word Wisdom* includes four week-long lessons, one each for using Context Clues, Root Words, and Reference Sources, plus a final review lesson that includes all the study words from the other three.

Zutell & Scharer (2007) have developed a variation of the TC3R structure to meet the needs of students in primary grades. Themes are built around young children's interests (e.g., animals, aspects of nature, author studies, recurring characters). Teachers select two or three picture books and/or children's poetry that fit the theme and also make good read-alouds. Units of study are briefer, lasting one or two weeks, and use a smaller set of focus words.

Activities begin with a read-aloud that focuses on enjoyment, understanding, and personal response. The focus on vocabulary begins on the second day with a modified Prediction Chart activity followed by a second read-aloud of the same text. Carefully guided by the teacher, the group revisits the Prediction Chart several times during and after to check and revise predictions, using context and base word clues. It's helpful to have an informative, easily accessible primary dictionary (e.g., *Merriam-Webster's Primary Dictionary*, 2005) available for you to model how to check meanings and to begin to develop your students' dictionary skills. For independent activities, children might listen to the story at a listening center, choose to illustrate one or more words, or match study words with an appropriate picture.

On other days, you might read texts on the same theme that both reinforce the previously introduced vocabulary and add new items to the list. You can also use a group dictation or interactive writing activity to create a list of synonyms for some of the focus words (e.g., for *sleep*: *doze, nap, snooze, napping*) or to expand a base word by adding familiar suffixes and prefixes (e.g., from *sleep*: *sleepy, sleepiness, sleeper, sleepier, sleepiest, sleepless, asleep, sleepyhead, slept*). Using the new words introduced through the readings and familiar words that fit the theme, the group can build

Concept Web for Sleep

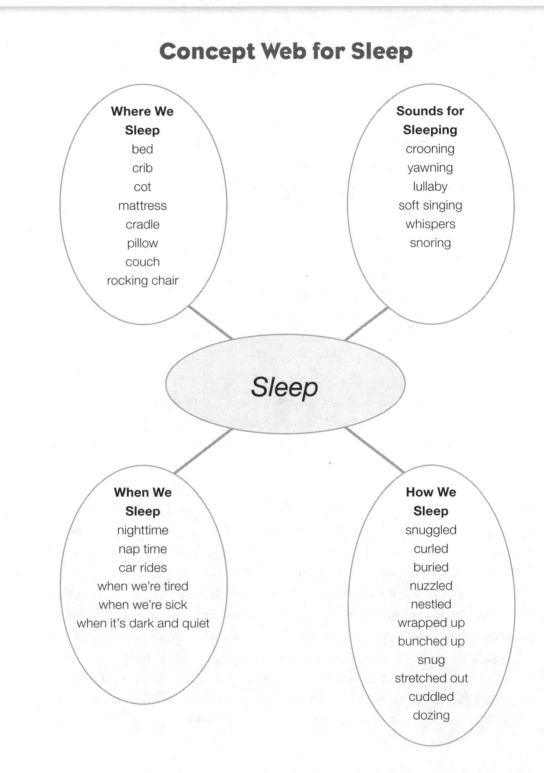

Where We Sleep
bed
crib
cot
mattress
cradle
pillow
couch
rocking chair

Sounds for Sleeping
crooning
yawning
lullaby
soft singing
whispers
snoring

Sleep

When We Sleep
nighttime
nap time
car rides
when we're tired
when we're sick
when it's dark and quiet

How We Sleep
snuggled
curled
buried
nuzzled
nestled
wrapped up
bunched up
snug
stretched out
cuddled
dozing

a Concept Web organizing key ideas and vocabulary. Revisiting the readings, charts, and maps throughout the unit serves as an ongoing form of review and reinforcement. Writing or dictating individual stories on the theme using the new vocabulary gives students the opportunity to connect the words and concepts to their own experiences.

The Final Word: If you think about your own vocabulary learning, you will find that you learn word meanings through context (hearing and using words in authentic language), your knowledge of word parts (roots, prefixes, and affixes), and reference (you look the word up in a dictionary, or someone tells you the meaning of the word). TC3R is a lesson framework that gives students practice in using all three strategies to determine meanings of unfamiliar but important words.

Books for Theme on Sleep

Dotlich, R. K. (1996). *Sweet Dreams of the Wild: Poems for Bedtime*. Honesdale, PA: Boyds Mill Press.

Goodman, J. E. (1999). *Bernard's Nap*. Honesdale, PA: Boyds Mill Press.

Purmell, A. (2003). *Where Wild Babies Sleep*. Honesdale, PA: Boyds Mill Press

strategy

Vocabulary Visits

What: Research tells us that perhaps the best way to develop our vocabularies is through direct experience. In schools, this often involves taking field trips. Camille Blachowicz and Connie Obrochta have described an excellent, extended vocabulary-building activity called Vocabulary Visits that takes the notion of a field trip to another level (Blachowicz & Obrochta, 2005). In this activity, which was developed by a reading specialist and her colleagues in order to expand their students' content vocabulary, teachers use a set of read-aloud books organized around a theme along with a poster and other visuals to create a "virtual field trip" (p. 262). Students engage in a variety of reading and writing activities to support vocabulary learning as part of the visit.

Why: At-risk students often have had fewer concrete experiences that support learning content-area concepts and vocabulary. And since students with limited vocabularies tend to learn fewer new words incidentally or on their own, they need focused, guided instruction to make significant gains in word learning. The teachers that Blachowicz and Obrochta worked with had noted that their students returned from field trips with ". . . new ideas, new questions to pursue, and new vocabulary to use in talking and writing about their learning" (p. 262). But even in the best of times, schools and teachers do not have the resources to provide for the number of field trips and concrete experiences at-risk students would need to close the gap. Using Vocabulary Visits regularly provides a means of building content vocabulary by incorporating some of the advantages of good field trips, which include a strong content focus connected to the curriculum, multisensory experiences, a knowledgeable adult to explain and clarify, and follow-up with new concepts and terms (pp. 262–263).

Who: The teachers who developed Vocabulary Visits worked with first-grade students in a multiethnic urban school. But we think this is such a sound, powerful approach that we believe it can be used to great effect with students of any social or economic background throughout the elementary grades.

When: Vocabulary Visits are best used as a regular part of an elementary unit of study. A unit may well last two or more weeks with at least 10–20 minutes planned for guided instruction each day, but students will also be engaged in related activities, like independent reading and discussing and adding words to the poster throughout the day. A Vocabulary Visit is an efficient approach to instruction because the activity integrates content activities, vocabulary learning, and literacy activities into a single unit of instruction.

How: The following description is a summary and adaptation from Blachowicz & Obrochta's report of what their teachers used in constructing and implementing their visits:

Planning: Review standards for science and social studies for your own grade and later ones to identify a focal topic you wish to study in depth. Select a set of at least five trade books on the topic that can be used as read-alouds for the visit. There is now a considerably wide selection of fiction and nonfiction trade books written for primary and elementary grade students on a variety of content topics and at varying levels of difficulty. You may want to have books at different levels to meet the needs of all your students. These can be found online, in professional resources that list books for children, on publishers' book lists, and in school or classroom libraries. After selecting the books, review them and your curriculum guides to select a core vocabulary you want your students to learn from the visit. Finally, create a poster with engaging pictures related to the theme to encourage discussion (graphics and pictures can easily be obtained through a quick Internet search).

If, for example, you chose the topic of weather, core words might include *clouds, rain, snow, storm, hurricane, tornado, blizzard, forecast, wind,* etc., and pictures or other graphics could easily be found or drawn and attached to the poster.

Jump-Start: Start with a brief introduction to the topic and then ask students to tell you what they know about it. Next, direct your students to do a First Write— that is, to generate a list of all the words they know about the topic—and add this list to their personal folder. It serves as a pre-assessment and also provides you with some diagnostic information about each child's familiarity with and understanding of the topic.

Group Talk: Next, bring out the poster you've constructed and initiate discussion by asking students what they see. As your students describe the visual images you've provided, they will generate a number of important words that you copy on to sticky notes and add at an appropriate place on the poster. Blachowicz and Obrochta stress that the teacher has a critical role in guiding discussion by asking questions, providing explanations, and making suggestions in order to elicit the targeted vocabulary. You should also engage your students' senses, not only through what they can see, but also by touching, listening, and imagining, as appropriate. It is also your role to begin to organize the words into categories and relationships.

Read-Alouds: Next, begin the read-alouds for the books chosen for the theme. Blachowicz and Obrochta point out that these should be more like parent-child interactions than dramatic readings. Your role includes stopping to clarify points, asking questions at places where there may be confusion or important information presented, and guiding word learning. To encourage active listening, have students give a thumbs-up when they hear one of the new words you've discussed before. You may also need to reread a sentence when none of your students responds to a critical term. Readings are followed by discussions, adding new words to the poster, and teacher-guided sorting of words into meaning-based categories. This part of the activity ends with students writing about something they've learned or found interesting. After the read-aloud, place the book in the class library. Ask students to read at least one book a week from those on the theme.

Do read-alouds for each book. Keep the poster on a classroom wall or stand. Follow-up activities during the unit include revisiting the poster, adding new words and possibly re-categorizing them. For extension activities, Blachowicz and Obrochta recommend "…semantic sorting, word games, writing, reading new books on the same topic, and rereading the books the teacher has read" (p. 266).

Once all the books have been covered, students do two writing activities. As a culminating experience, have students pull together ideas from across the unit in the form of a student book, a report on a favorite book, or a discussion of several things the student found interesting in the unit. For a Final Write, students list all the words connected to the topic they now know. You can compare this list to the one from the First Write to gain an informal measure of each student's learning.

Variations and Extensions: While teachers use Vocabulary Visits when they are unable to take actual field trips, they may be able to enhance the sensory element by using simple props when they are available. For example, in a unit on weather students might observe, record, and plot the changing readings over time from a large thermometer and/or barometer placed inside and/or outside the school building. Older students may be able to watch or do simple experiments to substitute for ones they might see done at a science center. Many Web-based activities are also available for simulating real events.

There are many common elements between Vocabulary Visits and the Theme, Context, Roots, Reference, and Review (TC3R) procedure discussed in the previous section, especially Zutell and Scharer's (2007) adaptation of TC3R for primary-grade classrooms (pp. 63–65). We do think there are some adaptations from the primary TC3R that could enhance the effectiveness of a visit. Word work with a focus on meaning elements in words would fit nicely into the Vocabulary Visit framework. And incorporating a second read-aloud so that students can focus on ideas during the first and give more attention to specific words in the second could well add to the effectiveness of the vocabulary learning. On the other hand, a stronger focus on including a multisensory dimension and the inclusion of a Final Write may well strengthen the primary TC3R approach. In any case, we believe that both are powerful, effective techniques for building student vocabularies and worth your consideration as frameworks for your vocabulary instruction.

The Final Word: Have you ever gone on a vacation to a place you had never been before or attended an event for the first time? You probably returned from that experience with new words that were specific to that place or event. It was this observation about their students that inspired the developers of Vocabulary Visits.

The strength of the Vocabulary Visits activity lies in effectively and economically integrating vocabulary learning, virtual experiences, and field trips using authentic literature, thematic units of instruction, and multisensory experiences within the immediate boundaries of the classroom and school. Blachowicz and Obrochta reported that students who participated in Vocabulary Visits gained in knowledge and confidence as they worked with related vocabulary, were proud of learning more complex, technical words, and gained motivation from seeing how many new words they could learn by the end of the unit (p. 267). We are confident that using this activity regularly in your own classroom will give you similar results.

Vocabulary Prediction Chart

What: A Vocabulary Prediction Chart is an interactive, advanced organizer for focusing student attention on new vocabulary found during text reading. It can be used independently or as part of a vocabulary instructional framework. (See TC3R discussed on pp. 60–65.)

Why: Recent research (National Reading Panel, 2000) has indicated the importance of learning new word meanings to support comprehension and raise reading achievement. You need tools that engage students in attending to new/unfamiliar words and help them develop strategies for figuring out the meanings of those words.

Who: The Vocabulary Prediction Chart is typically used with large and small groups of students beyond the primary grades, though it can be adapted for use with children in the early grades.

When and Where: The chart is used during guided reading instruction as you and your students read together and discuss fiction and nonfiction selections. The activity can also be used by content-area teachers with readings from their subject area.

How: You will need to create a large chart for summarizing discussions and provide students with smaller copies of the same chart. Organize the chart into columns with the following headings (see example on p. 72): 1) Word or Phrase, 2) Before Reading: What Do I Think It Means? 3) After Reading: What Do I Think It Means Now? 4) Checking Sources: What Did I Find Out?

Select 5–10 key words from the passage—words that are important to the understanding of the passage, words that you feel may be unfamiliar to students, and words that contain roots and other word parts that may be generalized to other words. Students copy the words into Column 1 and fill in their predictions of word meanings in Column 2. When everyone is finished, you lead a brief discussion.

Students volunteer their guesses, and you and/or the group choose one or more predictions for each word and write them on the large chart.

You and your students then proceed with the guided reading lesson, often using the Before-During-After format found in many reading lessons. When you have completed reading and discussing the text, students fill in the third column, revising their predictions. Again, you lead the discussion, now focusing on what the students have learned about the words from reading them in context. You (and your students) should point out specific context clues and how to use them. You may also demonstrate how to apply knowledge of word structure (prefixes, roots, suffixes) and encourage students to do so themselves. Next, direct your students to check for more precise meanings using a dictionary, glossary, or other source. In the final part of the discussion they compare and contrast their own ideas with what they have found.

Variations and Extensions: Recent research shows that differences in breadth and depth of vocabulary knowledge between at-risk and average students develop early and are considerable by the end of third grade (Hart & Risley, 1995; Biemiller, in press). So it's essential to include systematic vocabulary instruction as a regular part of the curriculum in primary grades, too. Vocabulary Prediction Charts modified to meet the needs of primary-grade students can be a central part of that instruction. We have discussed the modifications on the TC3R framework (see pp. 63–65). These include: a) using themes, trade books, and vocabulary more appropriate for primary students, b) introducing the key text with a read-aloud and discussion before introducing the chart, and focusing on vocabulary during a second reading on the following day, c) incorporating discussion about context clues and base words with frequent, familiar affixes into work with the chart, and d) introducing the use of a primary dictionary when checking word meanings for the final column of the chart.

The Final Word: Prediction, or the making of a hypothesis, is a strategy that scientists use to learn more about their fields of study. When students are given opportunities to predict meanings of words, we are essentially asking them to apply a method of scientific investigation to their own word learning.

Vocabulary Prediction Chart

Word or Phrase	Before Reading: What Do I Think It Means?	After Context: What Do I Think It Means Now?	Checking Sources: What Did I Find Out?

Context Clues and a Meaning Context Strategy

What: As we read, if we come across a word we don't know the meaning of, we can often gain a good sense of its meaning from the words around it. These provide context clues to the word's meaning. There are several kinds of information that such clues may provide. Knowing specifically what to look for can make it easier to figure out what the clues can tell us. A Meaning Context Strategy is a set of steps for finding out as much as possible about a word's meaning using the words, phrases, and sentences around it. Systematically applying a few simple steps can greatly increase the amount of information that we gain about word meanings during reading.

Why: Students in third grade and beyond learn between 2,000 and 4,000 new words a year (Bauman, Kame'enui, & Ash, 2003). Clearly, direct instruction accounts for only a small percentage of these words. They learn the vast majority in the context of assigned and independent reading. But learning from context isn't automatic. Researchers estimate that the meanings of only 5%–15% of unfamiliar words are learned during any one reading (Nagy, Herman, & Anderson, 1985). Thus students need to be exposed to new words multiple times through wide reading to build up information about them. And so they also need the ability to use the context surrounding a word to discover as much about its meaning as they can.

Who: A full range of students can benefit from practicing a set of steps for gaining information about word meanings from context. Materials at a third-grade level and above are likely to include a number of new meaning vocabulary words. Students in these grades will find knowledge of context clues and a Meaning Context Strategy especially useful. In primary grades, students are more often using context to aid in the visual recognition of a word whose meaning they already know. Still, many books that primary-grade teachers choose for read-alouds contain interesting and sophisticated vocabulary. So students in the early grades can be taught to recognize new words when listening to stories, and they can be given some strategies for discovering their meanings as well.

When and Where: Set aside 15–30 minutes during your language arts block or content instruction time to introduce the clues and the strategy early in the school year. You will probably need to revisit these ideas over each of the next few days. During the year, briefly review the concepts at least every few weeks. Primary-grade teachers should regularly incorporate vocabulary discussion into their read-aloud activities.

How: Begin by creating a list of the kinds of clues you want to introduce and the steps you want your students to use as part of the strategy. The table on p. 75 includes some ideas about clues that we've used in working with teachers and students. Since several kinds are similar and a long list can be a little intimidating, you may wish to use a smaller list of clues to start with and then add other kinds of clues over time.

Here is a set of steps we've used to check for these clues:

Read the sentence with the unknown word and some of the sentences around it.

Look for context clues. For example, what definitions or descriptions can you find?

Think about the context clues and other information you may already know.

Predict a meaning for the word.

Check a dictionary to be sure of the meaning. Decide which of the meanings in the dictionary fits the context.

(From Zutell, 2005).

Kinds of Context Clues

What Kind of Thing or Action the Word Is
Setting her feet on the blocks, leaning forward with the tips of her fingers on the ground, every muscle ready, she *dashed* forward as the race began.

Things or Ideas Related to the Word
In the church, the parents, godparents, family, and friends gathered around the priest and baby for the *christening*.

What a Word Is Used for
The pile-driver *forcefully* slammed the iron beam deeper and deeper into the earth.

How Something Is Done
The *incessant* beating of the drums continued without a pause throughout the night.

Location or Setting
The broken stoplight, high walls on each corner, and the heavy flow of traffic in every direction made that spot a very likely place for a *collision*.

Synonyms (Descriptions/ Definitions)
The *deluge*, a great and heavy downpour of rain, continued for hours.

Antonyms
His meaning was not clear and easy to understand, but *obscure*.

What a Word Is Like
Like the regular rising of the sun each morning, his arrival just at dinner time was highly *predictable*.

What a Word Is Unlike
Unlike the sloppy, careless scribbles of his sister, his handwriting was very *meticulous*.

Adapted from Zutell, 2005

Have your list of clues ready to present to your students on a chart, overhead transparency, or PowerPoint. Begin a discussion by introducing the topic and asking students to offer some ideas about how the words around an unfamiliar word might help them figure out its meaning. Make a list of these ideas, and then compare it to your list of clues. Combine the lists, expanding or condensing the set to one that meets your students' needs and understandings.

Next, ask your students to suggest some ideas about how they would go about looking for and using these clues. "What would you do first?" "Then what?" As in the first part of the discussion, make a list of their ideas, compare it to yours, and develop a set of steps combining the two lists. It is helpful to have key words for each step (as in the list above) to make the procedure easy to remember. You can illustrate how to use the clues and steps with the cloze procedure described on pages 109–112.

Variations and Extensions: Blachowicz and Fisher (2002) suggest slightly different terms and steps for their strategy: **Look** before, at, and after the word; **Reason** by connecting what you know with what the author has written; **Predict** a possible meaning; **Resolve** or **Redo** by deciding if you know enough or if you should gather information from other sources (p. 27). Use the strategy you are most comfortable with and the one you think will work best with your students or devise your own.

Another variation is to replace Read and Look to Listen when working with primary-grade students and using a read-aloud format.

The Final Word: Information from context is only one source students can use to unlock word meanings. Sorting words into their meaningful parts (prefixes, roots or bases, and suffixes) can also provide useful clues. And students need to learn how to use dictionaries, glossaries, and other sources to check their predictions and conclusions. Your students will have the best chance of finding out and remembering a word's meaning if they put together all three sources of information rather than focusing on just one.

Thematic Idiom Collections

What: A Thematic Idiom Collection (TIC) is nothing more than a collection of idiomatic expressions organized around a particular theme and displayed for students on a Word Wall or in their personal word journal for easy reference, study, and use.

Why: Some of the most challenging words for students to learn and use are expressions whose meaning is metaphorical rather than literal—idioms. English language learners have particular trouble with idioms since they tend to take idiomatic expressions, such as "it's raining cats and dogs," literally. Because idiomatic language is often local, even native English speakers often have trouble with idioms, and students are less likely to ask someone to define or explain an idiom.

Yet knowledge of idioms is very important. Writers often use idiomatic expressions to make their writing more interesting, so students frequently encounter idioms in their reading. And because idioms create meaning, understanding of idioms is central to students' reading comprehension.

Idiom knowledge is also important for writing. Just as writers use idioms to make their writing more interesting, students who begin to use idioms in their own language will see their writing improve as well.

Who: Thematic Idiom Collections can be used at any elementary or middle school grade level. We recommend that they be used sparingly in the primary grades, but with each succeeding grade level teachers begin to do more and more with TICs.

When and Where: TICs are a great way to start off a week in word study. You and your students share a group of idioms tied to a particular theme, and then, throughout the week, you and your students make it a point to include those expressions in your oral and written language. We learn language by using it, and when students begin to use idioms in their own language, those expressions will become part of their personal knowledge structures.

How: The key to Thematic Idiom Collections is to have some good resources that you can rely on in creating them. We have found two sources that you can use to begin your study of idioms with students—one is a book, the other a website:

◆ *There's a Frog in My Throat: 440 Animal Sayings a Little Bird Told Me* by Loreen Leedy

◆ www.idiomconnection.com

Unlike other sources, both of these collections arrange the idioms by themes. The Leedy book is organized by animals and the website by a variety of themes, including body, business, and sports. (Other books on idioms can be found in the Selected List of Resources: Word Origins and Expressions on p. 142 and at Tim's website, http://www.timrasinski.com/?page=presentations.)

Making a TIC takes about 15–20 minutes. Start by choosing a theme for the week or month, let's say ducks. Then have students brainstorm or share all the expressions or words that they can think of that refer to ducks or something about ducks but that have a meaning outside of those animals that fly and go quack. If students cannot think of any (which is likely with younger students), go to your sources and choose several. Here are some that we found:

◆ She took to it like a duck takes to water.

◆ Odd duck

◆ Quack

◆ Lame duck

◆ If it looks like a duck, and walks like a duck, and quacks like a duck, it's a duck!

◆ Sitting ducks

◆ It's like water off a duck's back

◆ Lucky duck

◆ That's duck soup

- ◆ Better get your ducks in a row

- ◆ It's lovely weather for ducks

Post the duck idioms on the Word Wall display (students can also write them in their word journals) and then over the next several days or weeks find ways for you and your students to use the idioms in written and oral language. Can you think of instances or times of the day when you might use some of these expressions? At the beginning of the next week (or whatever time interval you think is most appropriate), go through the same routine using a different theme (e.g., baseball idioms).

Variations and Extensions: Students will have a ball finding ways to use idioms in their own language. If you want to take it a step further, though, at the end of the week have students (individually or in small groups) write a paragraph using as many of the idioms as they can. Have students share a few, and post the exceptional ones on the classroom wall for students to read on their own. Here's a paragraph that a student wrote using insect expressions:

> My name is Mantis. I had been praying and hoping for a vacation to Florida for months. Finally, vacation time had come. I have been busy as a bee getting ready for my trip. I was so bug-eyed over all the work I had to do that I began to spin like a spider. I had more things to do than ants on an anthill. I packed like cocoons into my suitcase. But my car, an old VW Beetle, was making chirping noises like crickets. It was the fly in my ointment, the worm in my apple. My mother, the queen of the hive, gave me her blessings along with a stinging lecture on the birds and the bees.

The Final Word: Word study should be fun and creative. When we immerse students in the kinds of language we want them to learn and allow them to play with that language in creative ways, they will take ownership of that language and use it to express their own meanings—both orally and in their writing. You may be surprised at how your students will take to this form of learning—like a duck takes to water. It will really knock your socks off—you'll be that impressed!

Concept Maps

What: A Concept Map is a graphic representation of a definition or meaning of a word or concept. The map allows students to consider the various aspects of a word's meaning. It also guides students in the creation of definitions on their own.

Why: Having students define words and concepts is not a bad activity. It only becomes boring, onerous, and unproductive when students are asked to write definitions directly from a dictionary. At best, in such an activity students are engaged in rote memorization.

Who: Concept Maps are excellent for use with all students. With younger students you may need to reduce or remove some of the features from the map in order to simplify it for students who may be overwhelmed by the complexity of the full map.

When and Where: Many teachers do a word of the day. Concept Maps are perfect for exploring this routine, but the maps also work remarkably well with words or concepts that may be unique to a particular subject area.

How: Literacy scholars often frown upon the ubiquitous assignment of having students look up definitions in a dictionary. Constructing the meaning of a word or concept can be quite productive, but the tedious task of looking a word up in a dictionary and then blindly copying the dictionary definition—a definition that often is not terribly helpful in providing a clear meaning—is a passive task of memorization.

We see the value of asking students to construct definitions for words, but to do so requires a guide—and to this end we feel that a concept map is an excellent resource to help students gain access to word meanings. Just as a street map provides a visual guide for negotiating your way through a large city or across the country, a concept map or guide is a visual support that helps students negotiate their way through various aspects of meaning in words. Below is a concept guide that we have used with students.

Concept Map

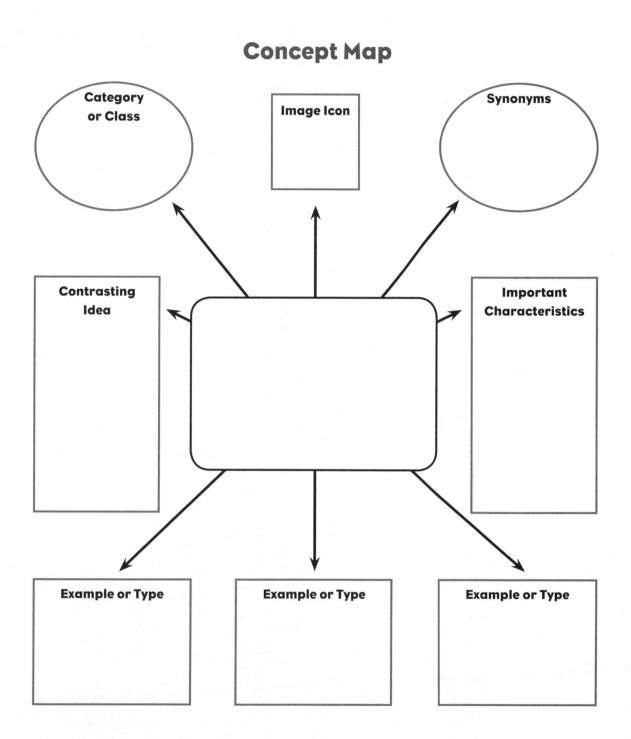

Category or Class

Image Icon

Synonyms

Contrasting Idea

Important Characteristics

Example or Type

Example or Type

Example or Type

As you can see from the map, we can determine a word's meaning in a number of ways by identifying the following:

◆ a meaningful category to which it belongs

◆ a logical contrasting concept

◆ a visual representation for the word

◆ synonyms

◆ key characteristics of the word

◆ examples or subcategories of the word or concept

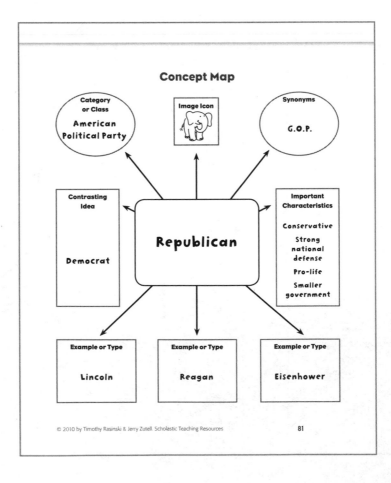

Concept Map

Category or Class
American Political Party

Image Icon

Synonyms
G.O.P.

Contrasting Idea
Democrat

Republican

Important Characteristics
Conservative
Strong national defense
Pro-life
Smaller government

Example or Type
Lincoln

Example or Type
Reagan

Example or Type
Eisenhower

81

A concept map works best with nouns that are familiar to students. Teachers who work with a word of the day can have students work in pairs, in small groups, or on their own to create a concept map related to these particular words. The concept map on p. 82 was developed by fifth-grade students for the word *Republican*, which they discussed during a recent presidential election.

A concept map frees students from simply copying and memorizing dictionary definitions and allows them to use their own background knowledge (and other resources) to create meaning. Interestingly, different students or groups of students often create maps for the same concept that look remarkably different. Comparing and discussing their concept maps will lead them to construct meaning on an even deeper level.

Variations and Extensions: Since the concept map we present on p. 81 is rather complex, it may not be appropriate for younger or less advanced students. The map can easily be adapted for greater simplicity by clipping certain elements of the map from a more complex one. For example, a map for younger students may only include the characteristics of the concept, or the exemplars, or the synonyms. Thus, if younger students were asked to create a map for the concept "dog," they might only include examples of various breeds of dogs, such as beagle, collie, and retriever. As students become more mature in their understanding of definition, the maps can become more sophisticated and complex in their presentation.

The Final Word: We have found that the regular use of a concept map will fundamentally change the way students view definitions. We often see students sketching a concept map on a piece of scratch paper when we ask them to define a word. The same is true for ourselves; when students ask us what a word or a concept means, the map pops up in our visual memory, and we will use it to create our own definitions of words.

Semantic Feature Analysis

What: In the previous section we described a Concept Map, a guide for students to use in defining one word or concept. Semantic Feature Analysis (SFA) is a guide for students to explore the meaning of several related words or concepts. In an SFA, students analyze each concept for characteristics (semantic features) that differentiate one word or group of words from the others. They then create definitions for these words by determining differentiating features and using those features to analyze or define the various words.

Why: Throughout their education, students are constantly exposed to groups of related words or concepts such as types of clouds, insects, flowers, triangles, the months of the year, important cities, American presidents, or land formations. Teachers want students to think like scientists. One thing that scientists do is analyze what they are studying to identify defining, differentiating, and common features. SFA guides students in thinking like scientists in analyzing words for defining characteristics.

Who: SFA is particularly helpful as students get into deep content-area exploration, but it is easy to adapt for students at all grade levels. Simply limiting the number of words and features used in the analysis is perhaps the easiest adaptation.

When and Where: SFA fits very well into content-area instruction, where students often explore several related concepts. It also fits easily into the word study component of your language arts curriculum. SFA allows you to present multiple words per day to students for critical analysis, which lends itself well to word-of-the-day activities.

How: The first thing that SFA requires is a visual grid or matrix, which can be easily made using the table function in your word processing program (see example p. 85).

Semantic Feature Analysis Form

Topic: _____

Columns = Words or Concepts   Rows = Differentiating Features

Topic:					

Next, think of (or have students think of) words or concepts related to a particular topic or theme and list them on the left-hand column of the grid. Then, working individually, in small groups, or as an entire class, students brainstorm a list of features that differentiate one or more concepts from the rest. The features should be stated in a way that can be answered with a yes or no. Once this is done, students complete the grid by filling in each cell with a *yes* or *no*, or a *plus* or *minus sign* (or a question mark if they are unsure of the answer). Once the grid is complete, students come up with a definition for each of the concepts. They can actually write the definitions or present them using the features they chose for their analysis.

Mr. Ramirez's fifth-grade class had just finished a study of American presidents. He had read several short biographies on presidents, and his students had independently done research on selected presidents and made oral presentations on their research. As a concluding activity, he had his students work in small groups doing a Semantic Feature Analysis. The students collectively brainstormed a set of presidents (Washington, Jefferson, Lincoln, Theodore Roosevelt, Wilson, Franklin Roosevelt, Kennedy, Nixon, G. W. Bush, and Obama.) Then, in small groups, the students chose features of the presidents to analyze. Finally, the students completed the grids. Mr. R reports:

Semantic Feature Analysis Form

Topic: _____

Columns = Words or Concepts   Rows = Differentiating Features

Topic: Presidents	President during a major war	War hero	From Virginia	Republican	Policies resulted in major social change
Washington					
Jefferson					
Lincoln					
T. Roosevelt					
Wilson					
F. Roosevelt					
Kennedy					
Nixon					
G. W. Bush					
Obama					

© 2010 by Timothy Rasinski & Jerry Zutell. Scholastic Teaching Resources

Essential Strategies for Word Study | **Part II: Exploring Word Meanings**   85

"It was interesting to observe the groups at work. There was a lot of good discussion going on in selecting of features. But then in the analysis phase, things really heated up. Some of the features were easy to analyze, but others really forced students to think and argue thoughtfully, and I might add passionately in some cases, for their analysis. One feature, for example, "Had policies that resulted in social change" promoted quite a discussion among group members. Arguably, all presidents had policies that resulted in change, but students were forced to think about the significance of the change and whether the change was positive or not. Then, when each group presented their features and analysis showing their grid on the document camera, I heard several students call out, 'We should have thought of that one,' or just plain 'Wow!' This activity really forced my students to think deeply and critically about presidents and the impact they had on America."

Variations and Extensions: We hope you can see many ways that SFA can be varied to work in your own classroom and in your own topic area. Groups can vary, topics can vary, and the analysis can be done at home or in the classroom. Here are two variations that we think are particularly valuable. When students first think of features, keep at least one column blank or empty. When students do an analysis using an initial set of features, they will likely find that two or more of the words or concepts share exactly the same features. When that happens, you can ask students to think of an additional feature or two that will differentiate the words that share the same initial features. Deeper and more critical thinking will be required.

As you and your students will find early on using SFA, students often choose features that cannot easily be analyzed using a yes-no response. Many of the features vary by degree and cannot easily be lumped into one category or another. As students become more aware of the nuances involved in analysis, you may wish to have them use a rating scale (e.g., 1 = yes, very definitely; 2 = yes, somewhat; 3 = could go either way; 4 = no, somewhat; 5 = no, definitely) for their analysis. This allows for greater flexibility as students think through and negotiate meaning with others.

The Final Word: SFA is a great tool not only for defining words but also for thinking and analyzing critically, as scientists do. Moreover, SFA involves comparing and contrasting a set of items that have something in common, a critical comprehension strategy. SFA will lead students to use compare-and-contrast in more productive ways and to reach a deeper level of comprehension in their reading.

strategy

Synonym/Antonym Word Ladders

What: Synonym/Antonym Word Ladders (SAWLs) or Semantic Gradients (Blachowicz & Fisher, 2002) are graphic organizers for teaching about the connections among a set of words and their meanings. In a Synonym/Antonym Ladder, the words represent different degrees along a scale related to a general concept or meaning.

Why: These Word Ladders are powerful tools for teaching students about the relationships among synonyms and antonyms. They help students learn about shades of meaning and choosing words that more precisely fit the ideas they wish to express. They provide a practical way of teaching students to use a thesaurus and other reference sources, and they build breadth and depth into students' vocabulary knowledge.

Who: All students can benefit from learning about word choice from the earliest grades. Formal instruction and regular use of Synonym/Antonym Word Ladders is appropriate for the upper elementary grades and beyond.

When and Where: Synonym/Antonym Word Ladders work best during focused vocabulary instruction, especially when you are teaching words around a theme, concept, or specific idea, or when working with a thesaurus or other reference sources that explore variations in word meanings.

Essential Strategies for Word Study | **Part II: Exploring Word Meanings**

How: Select a set of 5–7 words that represent degrees along a continuum for a specific concept (e.g., sound volume = *loud-soft*, time = *first-last,* visual intensity = *bright-dark*). A thesaurus is a good place to find a list of words related to a concept. Draw a visual display of a ladder or a stairway on a chart or whiteboard with at least enough rungs or steps for each of the words. Make copies for individuals or groups to work on. Insert two words on the ladder or stairway, usually at opposite ends. Provide oral and/or written directions to your students. Explain that some words can been seen as steps along a scale or continuum for a concept or idea and give one or two simple examples. Present the ladder they are to work on, then begin a discussion of the concept and explain the placement of the example words. Instruct your students to put the remaining words where they think they belong. Students can work individually or in small groups. As you lead a follow-up discussion, recognize that there can be good reasons for different placements—slightly different but acceptable interpretations of word meanings, closeness of meanings between synonyms, different but reasonable contexts for word use, and so on. Then have students check dictionary definitions when necessary.

The following example is a Synonym/Antonym Word Ladder that a teacher in the KSU Reading Clinic completed with fourth- and fifth-grade students:

Concept: Loudness

scream

shout

proclaim

state

mumble

murmur

whisper

Since students had already done several SAWLs and were familiar with the routine, the teacher presented pairs of students with all seven words and a blank ladder. The discussion between the student partners was quite interesting; although there was general agreement about which words dealt with loud and which dealt with soft, the actual placement on a particular rung led to quite heated exchanges.

More than one pair consulted the dictionary to determine the meaning of *murmur*. Clearly, these students were engaged in honing their understanding of the words. The teacher then put her version of the SAWL on a chart for display. Over the next several days, both teacher and students made it a point to use the words from the SAWL in speaking and in writing.

Variations and Extensions: Variations to SAWLs are many. Instead of using a ladder or steps to display the words, some teachers we know use a horizontal line to reflect the continuum of meaning. They call their version a Vocabulary Timeline. Several teachers note that the use of the timeline idea helps students solidify their understanding of timelines in social studies and number lines in math.

Once students have become familiar with SAWLs, rather than providing them with the words to be organized, you can simply given them the two ends of the continuum and have them think of and research words that might fit onto the ladder. This will necessitate using the thesaurus.

Another variation used in *Word Wisdom* (Zutell, 2005) is to provide two ladders side by side with one of them filled in with familiar and common words. Students then select from a list of study words (or words they find on their own) that match the words on the various rungs on the first ladder and place them on the second ladder.

Work with Synonym/Antonym Word Ladders transfers to critical reading and strengthens student word choice by adding precision and detail to their writing. To facilitate this transfer, teachers should work to make connections from this vocabulary activity to reading and writing. In all uses of SAWLs, we recommend that you keep the words that students have worked with on display for several days. (You may also wish to have students write them into their word journals.) Displaying the words on a Word Wall reminds you and your students to use these words. Words become anchored permanently in memory through meaningful and engaging introductions followed by regular usage.

The Final Word: Did you know that the word *thesaurus* is derived from the Latin and Greek words for *treasure*? (It's a great idea to talk about word origins or the stories behind words with your students— it makes them more memorable!) A thesaurus is a treasure of words—something of great value if you wish to write well. Though thesauruses are available in most classrooms, they are among the least used resources. SAWLs and their variations are great ways to get students into using their thesauruses.

List Group Label

What: List Group Label (LGL) is an approach to vocabulary teaching that goes beyond mere word brainstorming and has students engaging in a more scientific study of words. After students brainstorm a list of words, they organize the words in some meaningful way.

Why: Brainstorming words is a great way to get students to develop and think about a list of words related to a particular topic, but to get them to think more deeply about these words, we ask them to impose order on the words, much as scientists attempt to impose order on a seemingly chaotic world. Through the process of organizing the words in some meaningful fashion, the students are challenged to think about shared and differentiating characteristics of the words and the concepts they represent.

Who: LGL is appropriate for students at every grade level. The topics you choose for your students, of course, should match their developmental level and interests. With younger students you will have to provide more leadership and explanations in working through the words. However, through regular use, students will learn to apply LGL independently in their own learning.

When and Where: List Group Label works particularly well in subject areas that require students to do some reading. It works as a prereading activity, in which you assess and develop students' background knowledge. You can also use it after students have read or studied a particular topic in order to assess their learning and allow them to consolidate what they have learned.

How: Start with a topic your students will be reading about and studying—pollution, for example. Introduce the topic to students and allow for a brief discussion. Then ask students to brainstorm words related to the topic. Students can work individually, in pairs or small groups, or as a whole class. Display the words on the whiteboard or a classroom chart. You can elaborate on any words that you think may be unfamiliar. (This involves the "list" components of the lesson.)

The next step is the "group" and "label" component. Once you've established a list of words, ask students to think about how the words can be organized—are there some words that go together better than others? On another chart or sheet of paper, work with students to groups the words that have a shared characteristic and then develop a label that describes that group of words. In our pollution example, the labels that could be developed are "types of pollution," "causes of pollution," "results of pollution," and "solutions to pollution." Although this series of labels works well, there are several other options. The key is that there is more than one way to categorize, so students are forced to think deeply and creatively about words.

If you have students work in small groups on LGL, you will notice that they come up with different words on their initial brainstorm list and different ways of grouping and labeling the words. It is important for students to see the various ways that a list of words on a particular topic can be organized. Once they have organized a list of words, see if students can think of other words to add to the chart. Interestingly, once an organization is imposed on a particular topic, it becomes easier for students to think of additional words for a topic or subtopic.

If students do LGL prior to reading a text, they should now be ready to read. After reading, you can return with them to the LGL chart to add to it.

Variations and Extensions: With LGL, students create lists of the various groups of words, and the labels attached to them, on a chart or sheet of paper, but the activity can easily be extended into a more graphic form, with students making semantic webs that represent the groups. Imagine a visual chart in which the word *pollution* is at the center. Then, branching off from this center are the subheadings (labels) "types of pollution," "causes of pollution," "results of pollution," and "solutions to pollution," and from these subheads come the words that students have grouped under each subheading or label. We hope it's clear to you how this way of organizing words and concepts can easily be transformed into a traditional outline of main and subordinate ideas.

Because LGL is a way of organizing meaning, the activity can easily transfer into information writing. In our example above, students can write a paper on pollution in which each of the subheadings can become a paragraph or section of the essay.

The Final Word: Ginger Tolling, a fourth-grade classroom teacher, has the final word when it comes to LGL.

> In the past I often had students brainstorm words that came to mind when we began a piece of informational reading or a unit of study in a subject area. We talked about the words the students came up with, and then we moved on to the reading and our research. While this was a great start, I found that List Group Label allowed me and my students to take our brainstormed list to the next level. The organizing and labeling of the words we had brainstormed led to some interesting and engaging discussions that I know really prepared students for the reading and study of the topic.

strategy

Prevoke

What: Word study instruction helps students develop mastery over words—to learn the meanings of words as well as how to decode and spell them. These competencies are important because they are all involved in proficient reading. Word study can also function as a specific comprehension strategy. In "Prevoke," which also doubles as a comprehension strategy, students make predictions about a story or portion of a story using words that the teacher has selected. The name *Prevoke* is an example of "Be the Bard" (see pp. 50–52). Tim created the word by combing "pre" for prediction with "voke" for vocabulary: prediction based on vocabulary. Tim also thought that the term *Prevoke* sounds provocative.

Why: Mastery of words is important for reading proficiency; so is comprehension. Whenever you have an instructional approach that focuses both on words and on comprehension, you have powerful instruction. Prevoke is powerful instruction.

Who: Prevoke can be used at any grade level, although younger students will need greater support in negotiating their way through the activity. With regular practice, however, even young students will develop a remarkable level of independence through Prevoke. The strategy works best with materials that are narrative or story-like in nature.

When and Where: It's best to introduce Prevoke during a read-aloud period, where you can explain various elements of the activity as you read to your students. Once students get the hang of it, Prevoke works very well in guided reading, where students in small groups read and discuss trade books or stories.

How: Prepare for Prevoke by previewing a story (or a portion of a story) that you will be reading to your students, or that they will be reading on their own, and selecting words (or short phrases) that are essential to the meaning of the story and that may help to elicit wonderings about the nature of the story. Ten to 15 words seem to be an ideal number. Put the words on display for your students to view. Be sure to display them in the order in which they will appear in the reading.

The next step in Prevoke is to make sure the students have some understanding of the words and phrases. Review the words with your students and provide friendly definitions and descriptions for those they do not know or that you think they may have difficulty with.

Once students have a basic understanding of the words, have them manipulate the words in some way, such as sorting them into various semantic categories. The chart below reflects categories we have used in the past (the categories often depend on the nature of the story and the words that you choose).

Students can also sort words into categories of their own choosing (an open word sort). It's interesting to see the variety of creative ways students organize a set of words.

Sample of Semantic Categories for Word Sorting

- ◆ Setting Words/Character Words/Problem Words/Resolution Words

- ◆ Words That Evoke an Emotional Response/Words That Don't

- ◆ Powerful Words/Weak Words

- ◆ Kid Words/Adult Words/Both

- ◆ Pairs of Words That Somehow Go Together

Students work on their own or in small groups to sort the words. There are no correct or incorrect answers. Students can put the words into any category they like, as long as they can justify their choices and explain their thinking. We are not looking for correct answers, just good thinking.

As students manipulate the words in step 2, they usually find themselves beginning to formulate the words into the beginnings of a story. In the third step, by far the most engaging of all the steps, students finish the process. Individually or in small groups, they predict the story itself, using the words as the basis for their prediction. The words are presented in the order in which they appear. As students become familiar with the elements and sequence of narratives, knowing the order of the words can be a big help.

Once students write or share their predictions with classmates, they are ready to read the story on their own or hear it read to them by their teacher. The reading can stop at points in the story where students can update and refine their predictions.

The Three Steps of Prevoke

1. Introduce key words

2. Manipulate/sort the words

3. Predict the story

Once they have read the story, students can discuss how it relates to their predictions. They can compare and contrast the story with their predictions—which parts in both were the same, which parts were different. Although it is very difficult to accurately predict a story from a limited set of words, students enjoy the opportunity to try, and reading to confirm or disconfirm their predictions helps keep them engaged in the text. Students' predictions are seldom completely accurate, but sometimes their predictions form the basis of a story that may be better than the one they just read. In that case, you can ask students to flesh out their own predictions into a full-blown story!

Variations: There are many ways to vary Prevoke. Instead of presenting the words in order of their appearance, you can randomly present them to students on a chart. Some teachers call this Word Splash and Story Impressions. Instead of using words, you can give students sentences from the story that can be used to make predictions. While Prevoke works well at the beginning of a story, you may also choose to use it after your students have read a few pages, or even a few chapters, of a book. More background to a story results in better predictions. You may also choose a few words that we call *red herrings*—words that appear to have a high emotional or aesthetic impact but really are incidental to the meaning of the text. Students see how certain well-chosen words or phrases can have a powerful impact on how one interprets a story. The key to Prevoke and its many variations is to get students actively involved in making or constructing meaning. If comprehension is the active process of constructing meaning from printed words, then Prevoke is an excellent strategy for fostering comprehension among your students.

The Final Word: Perhaps the power of Prevoke can best be illustrated by a student teacher named Thomas who, because his cooperating teacher was ill, was responsible for a classroom of eight students identified as emotionally disabled. He had incredible difficulty keeping these students on task all morning. In fact, the students were so disruptive that Thomas felt like calling in sick himself for the afternoon. In desperation, he developed a Prevoke for one of the stories that was in the students' literature anthology. "Mr. Rasinski, it was like night and day! These students were so involved in trying to predict the story they were about to read, then reading it on their own, and then discussing it with me when they were done reading. They were really reading and really learning. This did it for me. Prevoke is definitely in my tool box of instructional strategies that I know work!"

Possible Sentences

What: Prevoke is a vocabulary and comprehension strategy that works very well with narrative texts. Possible Sentences (PS) is Prevoke's counterpart for information texts. In Possible Sentences, students work with a set of words from a passage they will be reading, but instead of predicting an entire story or story segment from the words (informational texts normally are not in the form of stories), students make predictions about individual bits of information from the given words. We often ask students to use a passage's content to predict the meaning of words. In Possible Sentences, we ask students to use words and their meanings to predict the content of a passage.

Why: The heart of the scientific method is the making of a hypothesis. Scientists attempt to predict the outcome of an experiment or an event in the natural world from limited information. Reading is a scientific activity; a good reader makes predictions or hypotheses about the meaning of a text while reading. Possible Sentences guides students in making hypotheses about what they will be reading.

Who: Possible Sentences can be used at any grade level; however, as with Prevoke, younger students will need greater support in negotiating their way through the activity. With regular practice, however, even young students will develop a remarkable level of independence in doing the activity. The strategy appears to work best with materials that are informational in nature.

When and Where: Since Possible Sentences works best with informational texts, it is ideal for use as an activity prior to and after content-area reading assignments. It can also be used during read-aloud experiences where the material is an informational passage.

How: Like Prevoke, the initial step in Possible Sentences is for you to preview a text your students will be reading and to select key words (or short phrases) that are essential to the main idea and facts presented (see Possible Sentences form on p. 100). Put 10–15 words on display for your students to view, in the order in which they will appear in the reading.

As with Prevoke, the first step is to introduce the topic of the reading to students using the words you have chosen. Provide student-friendly definitions that fit the context of the reading. Allow students to elaborate on your definitions.

The next step is the critical one. Ask students to develop three to five conjectures or predictions about what it is they will be reading. Each sentence must contain at least two words from the list of words you just presented. By asking students to use two words in each sentence, you are essentially asking them to develop a semantic relationship between the concepts. Research tells us that one of the best ways to learn words and concepts is to place them in relation to one another.

Students' sentences do not need to be true (after all, they have not yet read the passage), but the information in the sentences might be true; consider them predictions or hypotheses about the content to be read.

In a third-grade classroom, Mrs. Stewart prepared a PS lesson in advance of her students reading a passage on bears. Words she chose included the following: *bears, grizzly, brown, black, pack, omnivores, cubs, hibernate, forest, nocturnal, mammal, endangered species, wolves.*

Students worked with partners to develop four possible sentences. The following were among those that the students created:

◆ Brown bears are an endangered species.

◆ Grizzly bears live in packs.

◆ Bears hibernate because they are nocturnal.

- All bears are omnivores.

- Wolves are an enemy to bears.

Once students develop their sentences and share them with the class, they are ready to engage in reading. The purpose of the reading is to determine the veracity of their sentences. Students' wonderings and questions guide them in this reading.

When they have finished reading, students return to their statements and answer whether or not their sentences are true, based upon what they have read. Students can answer yes or no, or put a question mark next to each sentence about which they are unsure. These statements are similar to the kind often found at the end of a chapter of informational text. The main difference is that the questions are the students' own, not those of the teacher or the author of the passage; this provides students with a sense of ownership of their reading.

Variations and Extensions: Many possible variations to Possible Sentences exist. Having students sort the new words into semantic categories is an excellent way to get them to think more deeply about the words. You may also wish to have students rewrite the sentences that the reading proved false to make them true. This will keep students from holding on to an untrue understanding of the passage. Finally, the sentences that students were unable to verify can be the jumping-off point for further discussion and research.

The Final Word: After Mrs. Stewart's class developed and shared their sentences, the students eagerly read the passage. They really wanted to determine whether or not their predictions were true. Moreover, the discussion that followed the reading required little guidance from Mrs. Stewart. She simply made reference to some of the particularly salient sentences they had created, and the students took over. Mrs. Stewart commented on the power of Possible Sentences, "I think that Possible Sentences works because it mirrors what we all do when we read informational passages—we read to answer our own questions. Through Possible Sentences, we are showing students how to become good readers of informational texts."

Possible Sentences

Topic: _____

Key Words			

	True	False	Sentences
1.			Possible Sentence: _____ Corrected Sentence: _____
2.			Possible Sentence: _____ Corrected Sentence: _____
3.			Possible Sentence: _____ Corrected Sentence: _____
4.			Possible Sentence: _____ Corrected Sentence: _____
5.			Possible Sentence: _____ Corrected Sentence: _____

Essential Strategies for Word Study | **Part II: Exploring Word Meanings**

Extending Word Knowledge

The activities in Part III provide additional opportunities for students to add to their collections of words and to develop mastery over and fluency with the words they are learning. The activities provide interesting and enjoyable ways for students to examine and practice the words they are studying.

Word Walls and Word Banks

What: A Word Wall is a visual display of words that you want students to learn and master. Word Banks are individual sets of words for learning that students keep in a journal, on a deck of blank cards, or in some other form. Word Bank words can be drawn from the classroom Word Wall so that each student has the same words, or they can be chosen individually so that each student has a unique set of words.

Why: If you are going to teach words, they need to be easily accessible to students. Word Wall displays are easy for students to see, and they give teachers plenty of opportunities to practice those words with students.

Who: Word Walls and Word Banks are appropriate for any student who is in the process of learning words—that is, all students. Moreover, Word Walls can and should be used in every content area in which there is a specialized vocabulary.

When and Where: Word Walls are charts or other forms of visual displays that are hung from classroom walls. Word Banks are a personal set of words that students keep in a journal.

How: Let's say you have ten words you want to focus on for a week. Those words can come from reading, spelling, or any subject area. You introduce the words to students at the beginning of the week by using a marker to write them in large letters on a sheet of chart paper. Read through the words with students and share the meaning of the words

Practice the words with your students throughout the rest of the week. Read them first thing in the morning, read them before and after morning recess, read them before and after lunch, read them twice more at the end of each day. Read the words in different directions—top to bottom, bottom to top, left to right, or randomly as you point to the words. In addition to reading the words orally as a group, spell the words out loud with students; do it as a chant. Use the words repeatedly as you speak with students, making sure to draw attention to the words as you use them; encourage students to use the words in their oral and written language as well. Have students add the words to their own personal Word Banks for personal practice and use.

At the end of the week, you can hold students responsible for the words by using them in a vocabulary or spelling quiz.

If you have students use their Word Banks for words they select on their own, find opportunities for students to select and add four or five words to their Word Banks. This can be immediately after Sustained Silent Reading, after reading groups, or perhaps you can remind students to select words after a subject-area instruction or even at the end of the day, when students have a chance to reflect on all they have learned and covered.

Variations and Extensions: There are many ways to vary and extend Word Walls and Banks. First, by location—Word Walls do not have to be located only in the classroom. They can be also be located in the hallway, in the lunchroom, in the art room, in the media center, even right outside the bathrooms so that students can practice words as they line up and wait to use the bathroom. You can make Word Walls (or word folders) for parents to practice the words at home with their children.

A second way Word Walls can be varied is by the words you choose for your wall. Word Wall words can consist of high-frequency words (see p. 104), word families (see p. 43), word derivations (see p. 47), and words harvested by students after a read-aloud or shared reading (see p. 125). Smaller Word Walls can be devoted to words with particular syllables, vowel or consonant sounds, spelling patterns, prefixes, or suffixes.

Word Wall work can also be extended by what you have students do with the words. In addition to daily practice with the words, you can have students sort or categorize them (see pp. 39–42), play games with the words (for example, see pp. 127–131), and use the words in concept maps (see pp. 80–83). Various forms of practice and extension will surely make students more aware of the structure and meaning of whatever words you share through Word Walls and Word Banks.

The Final Word: Although practicing words may not seem like much fun, a certain amount of practice is necessary for words to get into one's memory. The fact that Word Walls invite communal practice and use makes the daily practice of important words quick, easy, and *fun*. We like to think of Word Walls as billboards for words—they are open invitations for students to view, analyze, learn, and use words that you and your students determine are important!

strategy

High-Frequency Words

What: Certain words appear often in students' reading. Words such as *the, it, my,* and *should* appear over and over again on the printed page. We want students to learn to instantly recognize these high-frequency words as soon as possible in their school lives. The first 300 words of Edward Fry's Instant Sight Words (see pp. 105–107) represent approximately two-thirds of all the occurrences of words that children and adults will encounter in their reading.

Why: By their very nature, high-frequency words should be words that students learn to recognize accurately and automatically. And because many high-frequency words are not phonetically regular, they often cannot be sounded out. For example, using phonics generalizations to pronounce a word like *said* would lead to an incorrect pronunciation. Therefore, students need to learn to recognize such words quickly and easily, without the need for word attack.

Who: We believe that by the end of second grade, students should have Fry's 300 Instant Words mastered to the point of instant and automatic recognition. We all know, however, that many struggling readers do not achieve this goal. These students require continuing instruction.

Fry Instant Sight Words
First 100 Instant Words

the	had	out	than
of	by	many	first
and	words	then	water
a	but	them	been
to	not	these	called
in	what	so	who
is	all	some	oil
you	were	her	sit
that	we	would	now
it	when	make	find
he	your	like	long
was	can	him	down
for	said	into	day
on	there	time	did
are	use	has	get
as	an	look	come
with	each	two	made
his	which	more	have
they	she	write	from
I	do	number	their
at	how	no	if
be	will	way	go
this	up	could	see
or	other	people	may
one	about	my	part

From Fry, E., Kress, J., & Fountoukidis, D. L. (2000). *The Reading Teacher's Book of Lists*, 4th ed. Englewood Cliffs, NJ: Prentice-Hall. Reprinted with the permission of Edward Fry, copyright holder.

Fry Instant Sight Words
Second 100 Instant Words

over	say	set	try
new	great	put	kind
sound	where	end	hand
take	help	does	picture
only	through	another	again
little	much	well	change
work	before	large	off
know	line	must	play
place	right	big	spell
years	too	even	air
live	means	such	away
me	old	because	animals
back	any	turned	house
give	same	here	point
most	tell	why	page
very	boy	asked	letters
after	following	went	mother
things	came	men	answer
our	want	read	found
just	show	need	study
name	also	land	still
good	around	different	learn
sentence	form	home	should
man	three	American	us
think	small	move	world

From Fry, E., Kress, J., & Fountoukidis, D. L. (2000). *The Reading Teacher's Book of Lists*, 4th ed. Englewood Cliffs, NJ: Prentice-Hall. Reprinted with the permission of Edward Fry, copyright holder.

Essential Strategies for Word Study | **Part III: Extending Word Knowledge**

Fry Instant Sight Words
Third 100 Instant Words

high	saw	important	miss
every	left	until	idea
near	don't	children	enough
add	few	side	eat
food	while	feet	face
between	along	car	watch
own	might	miles	far
below	close	night	Indians
country	something	walked	really
plants	seemed	white	almost
last	next	sea	let
school	hard	began	above
father	open	grow	girl
trees	beginning	mountains	river
never	life	four	cut
started	always	carry	young
city	those	state	talk
earth	both	once	soon
eyes	paper	book	list
light	together	hear	song
thought	got	stop	being
head	group	without	leave
under	often	second	family
story	run	later	it's
example	sometimes	took	keep

From Fry, E., Kress, J., & Fountoukidis, D. L. (2000). *The Reading Teacher's Book of Lists*, 4th ed. Englewood Cliffs, NJ: Prentice-Hall. Reprinted with the permission of Edward Fry, copyright holder.

When and Where: If students need to learn 150 words by the end of grade 1 and another 150 by the end of grade 2, that means that they need to learn five or six new high-frequency words per week, adding up to 150 words in 25 to 30 weeks of school. This leaves another six to ten weeks for additional review and practice. We recommend that students practice the words you introduce (as well as previously introduced words) throughout the school day and during the word study component of your language arts curriculum.

How: High-frequency words can be taught and practiced in many ways. First and foremost, plenty of reading will maximize students' exposure to these words. Students should have maximal exposure to silent, oral, and choral reading; individual, paired, and group reading; and stories, informational texts, poetry, and songs.

We recommend a High-Frequency Word Wall and Word Banks. Add five or six words per week to the Word Wall and practice the words in brief bursts with students at various times throughout the day (see pp. 102–109). Add the words to your weekly spelling list to foster spelling mastery. Play lots of word games with students using the high-frequency words—WORDO is a great game for practicing these words (see p. 112). Students can use high-frequency words placed on flash cards for brief but effective practice. Have students sort the words in various ways (see pp. 39–42), and include the words in word-building activities (see pp. 30–38, 121–124). Send the words home for more practice with Mom and Dad.

Parents are always looking for ways to help their children over the summer. At the beginning of the summer, send parents the high-frequency words students learned during the school year, along with the words they will be covering in the coming year. Provide parents with suggestions for games and activities that will help the children continue their high-frequency word learning. Imagine the advantage it will provide students to enter the school year already knowing a large body of words that will be covered in the coming year!

Variations and Extensions: While high-frequency words are generally taught in word lists, word-by-word reading is a sign of a lack of fluency. A solid body of research supports the idea that students should learn to read in syntactically appropriate phrases (Rasinski, 1994). A great extension of high-frequency word learning is to teach the words in phrases and short sentences as well as in isolation. Tim has put Fry's instant words in the context of phrases. (See his site at: http:// timrasinski.com/presentations/fry_600_instant_phrases.pdf). Having students practice five to ten of these phrases per week will help reinforce the words in a different way, and at the same time it will help students practice the words in meaningful phrases.

The Final Word: The fact of the matter is that when it comes to learning to read, some words are more important than others. For beginning readers, many of these words are high-frequency words. The very fact that you can give your students mastery of two-thirds of all the occurrences of words they will encounter in reading by teaching them 300 words tells us that high-frequency word instruction needs to be a key part of your daily word study instruction.

strategy

Cloze Texts and Activities

What: A cloze text is simply a passage from which words have been deleted. The task for the student is to determine the words that are missing by using the meaningful context of the passage. Although the cloze was originally developed as an assessment instrument, it can easily be adapted for use in word study instruction.

Why: Have you ever noticed that when you come to an unfamiliar word while reading, you are still able to figure out the word's meaning? Using the context of the passage, along with the first letter or two of the word, is often sufficient. Specially designed cloze texts provide an excellent approach for students to develop their own skill at using context in word recognition.

Who: Cloze texts and activities can work with students at any grade. It is important to ensure that the texts you use for cloze are at the students' instructional or independent reading levels.

When and Where: As a specific word work activity, a cloze can fit into your word study time. If, however, you create a cloze activity from a subject-area text, then the activity can be integrated into your content-area instruction. If you choose to do a cloze activity with your students, we recommend that you do it at least twice a week.

How: Cloze activities begin with a 100-word passage at your students' reading level. The passage can come from a familiar book or one they will be reading in the near future. Once you have selected the passage, make a copy of it. In previous years, we have simply copied the passage (usually a page or two from a trade book or textbook that the students have read or will be reading). With the advent of new technology, you can also copy the passage by scanning it and saving it as a document on your computer. Leave the first sentence intact, and then find words that you think can be determined from the context of the passage itself. Delete these words by scratching them out with a marker (if you are using a photocopied version of the passage) or electronically deleting them if you are using an electronic copy. (Be sure to leave a blank line, the length of the deleted word, in place of the original word.) If you think the first letters or letter combinations of some words may be helpful, you can leave the first letter(s) of those words in the text. In fact, you can leave in any letters that you choose (vowels, middle letters, last letters, etc.). You and your students will find early on that the most important letter when decoding words using context is the first letter. Below is a portion of an Emily Dickinson poem that we transformed into a cloze activity.

A bird came down the walk;

He did not know I saw;

He bit an angleworm in h _____ (1)

And _____ (2) the fellow, raw.

And then he drank a _____ (3)
From a convenient grass,
And then h _____ ed (4) sidewise to the wall
To let a beetle pass.

He gl _____ (5) with rapid eyes
That hurried all around,
They looked like frightened b_____ (6), I thought;
He stirred his velvet head.

Once you develop the cloze activity text, make copies for every student. The task is to determine the words you have deleted. Rather than sounding the words out (not all the letters are present to allow sounding), students will have to use the context, the length of the deleted word, and whatever other letter clues you have embedded into each word. Students can write their responses either directly into the text itself or onto a separate numbered answer sheet.

Once students have completed the cloze activity (by themselves or with a partner), check their responses with them; but more important, talk with your students about the thought process required to determine some of the deleted words. For example, the answer to no. 3 is *dew*. The reasoning required to get the correct answer was first to notice that in the first line the bird drank. The next line indicates that what he drank came from grass. What sort of liquid that is a relatively short word might you find on grass? The answer is, of course, *dew*. Not all students will be able to figure out the unknown words easily. Having students share their strategies and approaches will familiarize these students with the problem-solving methods that others have used, and they will begin to use the same strategies themselves. In this particular case, the clear insight to be shared with students is that if you come to a word you are not sure of, keep reading; often it is the context that follows the unknown word that is most helpful.

Variations and Extensions: Numerous variations and extensions to cloze activities exist. Here are two. If you work with younger students, you can create a group cloze activity by covering up words from a big book or chart story using sticky notes. For students who may find a cloze activity a bit too challenging, try using the maze procedure. The maze is simply a multiple-choice cloze. For each deleted word, provide three or more choices from which students choose the best answer.

Cloze activities work nicely in content-area reading. The procedure is the same—using a textbook or informational book passage, delete academic words from the content lesson you have just covered. This is a great assessment tool, but we think the real muscle behind cloze activities comes from using them instructionally—to build vocabulary and vocabulary problem-solving skills and strategies.

The Final Word: Good readers use all the tools at their disposal for determining unknown words—phonics, word patterns, word structure, and context. We know of no better activity for nurturing the ability to use context in word decoding and thereby improving vocabulary and reading comprehension among your students.

strategy

WORDO!

What: Most people, especially children, like to play games. WORDO is a simple game, a take-off on bingo, and a great activity for helping students review words they have previously learned in language arts or other content areas.

Why: As you have seen in this book, there are many great ways for students to learn and explore words. But it is through practice and review that those newly learned words become anchored within a student's memory. Review is important. The problem is making word review fun and engaging for students. Games are one way to make this happen.

Who: WORDO is a great game for students at any grade. It is important to use words that students are in the process of learning or reviewing. Additionally, you'll want to make sure that the number of words you use does not overwhelm the students. For students in grades K–1 use 9–12 words; grades 2–4, 16–20 words; and grades 5 and up, 25–30 words. Choose or make the WORDO sheet that best fits the number of words you use.

When and Where: WORDO is best used when you have about 20–30 minutes free to play a game with your students. It is a great review activity, so it works particularly well after you have completed the study of a topic which a number of words were covered.

How: WORDO is played much the same way as bingo. The first requirement is a WORDO card, which is nothing more than a 3" × 3", 4" × 4", or 5" × 5" grid. A reproducible 4" × 4" WORDO card is featured on p 114. You can make a WORDO card using the table function on nearly any word processing program. Duplicate a WORDO card for every student you will be working with.

The second and most important requirement is that you will need at least one word for each empty cell on the WORDO card, although we recommend that you have three to five more words than empty cells (when the number of words is the same as the number of empty cells, the odds increase that more than one student will win WORDO at the same time.) The important words can come from any source: a spelling list, a content area, Word Walls, etc. Display the words on a chart or whiteboard for all students to see.

Students then fill each cell with a word of their own choosing from the list. The goal is to have the words in each student's WORDO card arranged differently. Students may also choose one cell to mark as FREE. Once students have completed their cards, distribute markers (bingo chips, dried lima beans, etc.) to each student to cover each cell as each word is called.

In the typical WORDO game, the teacher acts as the master of ceremonies. In this role, you randomly choose a word from the list and call it out, or call out clues that allow students to determine the word you chose. (You can give the definition or

WORDO!

other structural clues. For example, for the word *triangle*, you might say, "This word begins with a consonant blend, has two syllables, and the last syllable rhymes with 'dangle.'")

Students fill out their cards with the marking chips until, as in bingo, they get a vertical, horizontal, or diagonal line filled or all four corners filled. When this happens, they call WORDO. You check their card, and if their game card is correct, they win a prize of some sort. Students then remove the marking chips from their cards and a new game begins. The excitement of winning the game and earning a prize is motivating, but beneath the game is solid practice in learning the words you want your students to know.

Variations and Extensions: If you are not fond of having students fill in a game card, WORDO can also be played with students' Word Banks if they are in the form of word cards (individual words written on an index card or some other card). When WORDO is played in this way, have students choose 9, 16, or 25 words from their Word Bank (the words in the Word Banks have to be the same for all students). Have them arrange their cards face up. This becomes their WORDO card. Then simply have students turn over the appropriate word card as the word or its clue is called out. Lines, diagonals, or four corners win the game. After a game ends, students can rearrange their word cards and replace them in order to make a new WORDO card.

The Final Word: Tim has used WORDO with students in all his teaching positions from first grade to college. When he worked as a substitute teacher, WORDO was always in his bag of teaching tricks, regardless of the students he was working with. "Kids love WORDO, in every grade level, and in every subject area for which there are words to be learned. If I couldn't determine what it was I was supposed to cover in the classrooms in which I was subbing, I found that I could always keep students engaged for at least 20 minutes, more like 30, with WORDO. They thought it was just a game. I know they were learning the words that were key to their understanding of whatever it was they were studying."

Flip Folder

What: A Flip Folder is a simple device for covering and uncovering spelling words as a student practices those words.

Why: Students use a Flip Folder to practice the list of spelling words from their weekly lesson or assignment. It is particularly useful because it supports independent practice and provides immediate feedback.

Who: Students at all levels who need to master a set of spelling words can use a Flip Folder effectively.

When and Where: After a group or individual spelling lesson (e.g., a DSTA, see pp. 21–27), a Flip Folder can be used during short periods of transition or free time during the school day or at home.

How: Flip Folders are available commercially, but they are easy to make using a manila folder as shown on p. 117. Turn the folder so the closed or creased end is up. Crease again along a line about an inch from the top. (Most folders have a pre-formed line ready for creasing.) Draw two vertical lines down from the crease, dividing the area into three equal sections. Cut along the lines to the crease and fold back each of the three sections at the crease. Close the three flaps you've made. Label the three sections: 1) Look-Say-Cover, 2) See-Write-Check, and 3) See-Rewrite-Check.

Practice Procedures: Older students use an 8.5"-by-11" page turned horizontally with lines drawn for each word. Lined writing paper works well for primary students. The paper can also be divided into three sections to match the folder sections. The student copies her spelling words into the first column, starting low enough so that the list begins below the crease. She then slips the paper into the folder and follows the procedures for each section, one word at a time. Guide

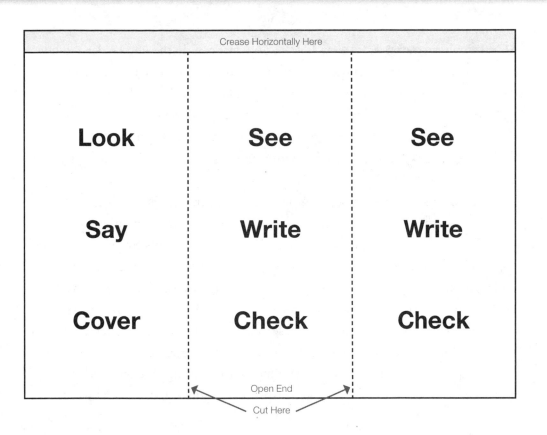

the student with these instructions: "Open the first flap, look at the first word, say it, then cover it with the flap. Now open the second flap. See the word in your mind and then write it. Check your spelling with the correct spelling under the first flap. Follow the same steps a second time, spelling the word again in the last column. Now follow the same steps for each word on the list."

A good procedure for checking a spelling is to use the Dot-Slash-Circle-Check Method, in which the student compares her spelling with the correct one, letter by letter. The student puts a dot under her letter if the letters match, places a slash where the letter should be in the case of an omitted letter, circles any wrong letters, and uses a checkmark to indicate that she has spelled the word correctly. This procedure helps focus the student's attention on how a word has been misspelled and what needs to be done to correct it.

Variations and Extensions: Students can do the Flip Folder activity independently or with a partner. It fits well as a word study center activity, where pairs of students work together through a Flip Folder over the week's words once a day or according to whatever schedule you deem appropriate. Some teachers we know use Flip Folders as a cross-grade activity where older students (especially struggling readers and spellers) work with younger students on the younger student's words.

Flip Folders also work well as a group activity. In this variation, each student writes the words in the first column as you dictate and write them on a chart. Then you cover the display of words that you made and have students cover their own first column. You dictate the words twice more, with students writing the words in the second and third columns. Students then check their own spellings against yours, and they can also track or chart their progress from the second to third spellings. Can students identify progress from the second to third columns? Students can also work in groups or teams to total their scores and compare scores with other teams.

Group practice of this sort is a great time for the sharing of mnemonic devices and other strategies for remembering the spellings of unusual or difficult words.

The Final Word: To be sure, Flip Folders provide a type of spelling practice, but the activity has a game-like feel and an air of importance. The Dot-Slash-Circle-Check method takes the activity beyond rote practice to foster students' ability to focus more clearly on *how* their spellings are different from the correct ones and *what needs to be done* to fix them.

Flip Folders can be used in combination with spelling games, practice tests, and other practice activities. They are also ideal for use at home. Parents love making Flip Folders with their children and using them regularly to practice the words.

Word Hunting

What: Word study activities encourage students to look carefully at words, with a focus on patterns that connect pronunciation, spelling, and meaning. Word Hunting extends that study by encouraging students to search in their memories and in their reading and writing for additional examples of words following similar patterns.

Why: Word Hunting expands the number of words students study from a basic set or list to a much larger number. It gives students a stronger sense of ownership by making a clear and direct connection between words used in formal study to words they rely on in their everyday activities. Word Hunting also provides a level of individualization to a word study activity; in searching through their own reading materials, students find words at their personal instructional level. Finally, in order to Word Hunt successfully, students must examine words in their readings and personal writings in closer detail, so they get useful proofreading practice.

Who: Word Hunting asks a student to work with patterns at his own instructional level and to take a close look at his own reading and writing, so students at any level can benefit from the activity.

When and Where: Word Hunting works well as a follow-up to a focused word study activity, such as Word Sorting (pp. 39–42) or Making Words (pp. 30–35), or as part of an instructional cycle like the Directed Spelling Thinking Activity (pp. 21–27) or Sort, Search, and Discover (pp. 27–30). Once you ask students to hunt for words of a particular type, the hunting can be done individually, in pairs, or in small groups. It can proceed for a specified time (usually 10–15 minutes) or as an ongoing activity, during "down time" at the beginning of the day, after lunch, at recess, or any other time there's "a break in the action." Word Hunting is also a great activity to do at home with the support of parents and other caregivers.

How: Word Hunting may appear to be a straightforward activity that requires little direction, but we have learned from working in classrooms and clinics that beginning and struggling readers and writers need additional instruction and demonstration in how to find words with specific characteristics.

We suggest you begin by tapping into the most available source—students' own knowledge and memory. We call this a "Brain Search." The easiest Brain Search is a simple rhyming task: changing the beginning letter, blend, or digraph. Demonstrate how to do this by taking a simple rhyme, -at, for example, and as you think aloud, go through the alphabet consonant by consonant, from *bat* to *zat*, keeping those items that are real, known words. Next, check the blends, beginning with *bl*, then *br*, *cl*, *cr*, etc. Last, do the common digraphs, *ch*, *sh*, *th*. Turn over control to the students gradually, as they get the idea. Have them pronounce the new combination and decide whether it's a real word or not. Use chart paper or a blank transparency to keep track of the real, known words you and your group find.

Next, move to finding words in print. Take a favorite reading selection and familiar pattern—*ing,* for example. Demonstrate how to slide your finger under the words, focusing your attention on the letters in the words as you search for a given letter combination. Use your nonwriting pointer finger. As each word is found, write it on a separate piece of paper.

As students find new words, they can add them to their lists, pattern by pattern, or put them on cards to add to their Word Banks for sorting. Students can also add them to a class Word Wall or to their individual word journals.

Variations: Word Hunting focuses on specific patterns or features. Harvesting Words, discussed on pp. 125–127, also involves hunting for words, but it is an open-ended activity that focuses on words that strike the reader as new and interesting. Both ways of collecting words provide important opportunities for students to be actively engaged in expanding their word knowledge.

The Final Word: Hunting and gathering has been an essential human activity from earliest times. In modern societies, we no longer hunt to sustain ourselves as we once did, but we do often hunt for items as part of everyday living. Effective searchers often have a strong sense of purpose, a clear mental picture of what they are looking for, reasonable familiarity with the terrain, and a systematic plan for hunting efficiently. As with most complex skills, putting all these things together takes considerable effort at first. It may be difficult to separate our target from its background. But with greater knowledge and regular practice, we learn to sort things out more easily and efficiently, and our skills of observation and detection become sharper. So it is with words and patterns. (Think about how hard it would be to locate a particular Chinese character in a page of such characters if you do not read Chinese, compared to locating an English word in a page of familiar print, even if that word differs only slightly from those around it.) Word Hunting builds students' powers of observation and detection and their sensitivity to word forms and patterns. It also gives them the opportunity to take pride in what they have found.

strategy

Word Ladders

What: A Word Ladder is a game-like word-building activity in which students, guided by the teacher or on their own, start with one word and build a series of new words by changing one or two letters.

Why: Research tells us that students learn by actively manipulating the task or concept to be learned. The learning is particularly powerful when a teacher guides students through the process of manipulation. Moreover, we also know that games and game-like activities engage students' interest.

Who: Word Ladders are appropriate for students at any age. The key is to use age-appropriate words.

When and Where: Word Ladders fit well into the word study component of the literacy curriculum, but since they only take a matter of minutes to complete, many teachers find time to do Word Ladders at the beginning or end of the day or during breaks that crop up within the day. Because Word Ladders can be done independently, they also fit very well into a word study center.

How: To develop a Word Ladder, start with a word you wish to teach. Then add, subtract, change, or rearrange one or a few letters in the word to come up with a new word. Do the same to the second word, and so on until you have made 5 to 12 words. A challenge is to try to make the last word you made somehow related to the first. Once you have your words, think of meaningful clues that will help students determine the words as you lead them through the Word Ladder. Below is a Word Ladder that we created for Halloween:

1. trick   Change one letter in *trick* to make something that trains ride on.

2. track   Change one letter in *track* to make a word that describes when you make a copy of a drawing by putting a transparent sheet of paper on top of a picture and then copying the outline of the drawing.

3. trace   Change a letter in *trace* to make a word that is a prayer that some people say before meals.

4. grace   Change a letter in *grace* to make a word that describes what your mother does when she shreds cheese for pizza.

5. grate   Rearrange the letters in *grate* to make a word that is a homophone for *grate* but means grand or terrific.

6. great   Change a letter in *great* to make a word that goes with word no. 1 and is something you do on Halloween.

7. treat!

Once you have developed your Word Ladder, have your students number vertically on a blank sheet of paper from 1 to 7; have them write *trick* next to number 1. Then lead them through the process of building the next six words in the list.

Variations and Extensions: Tim has worked with Scholastic to develop a series of Word Ladder books. These books contain individual lessons that can be duplicated for students in your class. You can do them with students or, once they get the hang of how Word Ladders work, they can do them independently at their desks or in the word study center. See p. 124 for a reproducible sample.

Students can develop Word Ladders of their own and then lead classmates in the same activity. You can also think of two related words that you know can be developed into a word ladder (e.g., *first* to *last*) and challenge students to make their own Word Ladder that begins and ends with those words.

What's Next? Have students choose five or so particularly interesting words from a completed Word Ladder to add to the classroom Word Wall or to their personal word journals or Word Banks. Encourage students to use these words in conversation and in their writing. Once they have added ten or more words to the wall or Word Banks, students can sort the words in various ways and use them in other word games.

The Final Word: We have used Word Ladders with children and teachers for years. Kids love doing them. They also love making them. Teachers love them too. After Tim did a Word Ladder with a group of teachers a few months ago, one teacher commented that they reminded her of crossword puzzles for kids: each word has a clue, numbers of letters are indicated, and the words are interlocked. Almost immediately after that teacher shared her comment, another teacher raised her hand and added, "That lady is right; and I don't know anyone who likes to do crossword puzzles who doesn't have a large vocabulary, is not a good speller, and is not a voracious reader!"

Name _____

Read the clues, then write the words.
Start at the bottom and climb to the top.

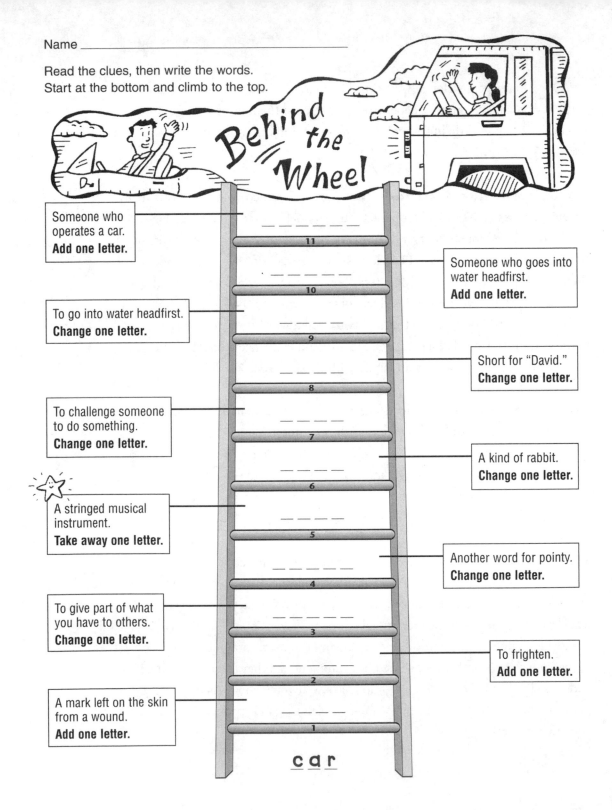

Behind the Wheel

Someone who operates a car.
Add one letter.

Someone who goes into water headfirst.
Add one letter.

To go into water headfirst.
Change one letter.

Short for "David."
Change one letter.

To challenge someone to do something.
Change one letter.

A kind of rabbit.
Change one letter.

A stringed musical instrument.
Take away one letter.

Another word for pointy.
Change one letter.

To give part of what you have to others.
Change one letter.

To frighten.
Add one letter.

A mark left on the skin from a wound.
Add one letter.

11
10
9
8
7
6
5
4
3
2
1

c a r

Harvesting Words

What: Books are some of the best sources of words. Authors deliberately use words that they feel will engage their readers. Some people call these literary words; others call them Tier 2 words (Beck, McKeown, & Kucan, 2002). Regardless of what they are called, they are some of the most important words for students to learn because they appear with great frequency in the books they will be reading.

Word Harvesting is an activity in which students select words to learn from materials they read or that a teacher reads to them. In a friendly manner, the teacher or other students help to define the words, then the words are put on display and students are encouraged to use the words in conversation and in their writing.

Why: For students to develop an appreciation of words, they need to notice the wonderful words that others use in their own language. Authors, poets, and others who write for a living use words with skill and purpose. When we ask students to become aware of words that authors and other writers use, we foster an appreciation for the way that authors *use* words. Students become word connoisseurs, and they begin to use these words in their own language.

Who: Word Harvesting is perfect for students at any age, as long as the books and other reading materials are age-appropriate.

When and Where: Harvesting words fits seamlessly into any reading activity that students already do. It can happen during guided reading, sustained silent reading, or group oral reading. We think it works particularly well during the daily read-aloud period when the teacher reads books and other materials to children that they may not read on their own.

How: The activity is really quite simple—whenever students read on their own or when material is read to them, simply ask them to notice the interesting words that the author uses in his or her writing.

The example we share comes from a read-aloud. When the teacher reads to students, she asks them to listen attentively and to "be on the lookout" or "listen out" for interesting words that the author uses. You'll only need to read a few pages before students will have a host of words to share. You may also have to read the first few pages twice—the first time to harvest words, the second time to enjoy the story itself.

Once the read-aloud session is completed, ask students to call out five words or so they thought were interesting. As they call out the words, you or a student can write them on the classroom Word Wall (see pp. 102–104). Students may also enter them into their personal Word Banks or journals. The words are on display as a reminder for students (and for you) to use them in speaking and writing over the next several days.

After reading just the first few pages of *Officer Buckle and Gloria* (Rathman, 1995) first graders in Ms. Winters's class called out the following words:

swivel chair, bulletin, thumbtack, banner, announced, stared, attention

After Ms. Winters wrote the words on the Word Wall, she briefly talked about the meaning of each word and asked students to add their own insights. Then, throughout the remainder of the day and into the next few days, she used these words purposefully. Ms. Winters made announcements of bulletins to the class, stared at students who were not paying attention to their word, and thumbtacked a banner over the bulletin board. She also made it a point to use the words in the public writing she did on the whiteboard and overhead projector. Students noticed her use of the words and began using the words themselves.

Variations and Extensions: Word Harvesting can also be done with poetry, songs, and other texts that students may read as a group. If you do Word Harvesting daily, and your students harvest six words a day, they will have harvested over a thousand words in the course of a 180-day school year.

In some classrooms we have visited where Word Harvesting occurs, students have chosen so many words that the charts or displays of words have gravitated into the hallway. A banner outside Room 106 proclaims, "Look at the Words Room 106

Has Learned This Year!" Students there began and ended each day chanting together some of these words, led by their teacher. Students in other classrooms began to notice the powerful words that the kids in room 106 had learned, and before long several classrooms had developed their own word harvesting routine!

The Final Word: Tim has used Word Harvesting in his reading clinic for years. Perhaps the most telling evidence of the power of Word Harvesting came one day when a mother of one of the students stopped by to talk with Dr. Rasinski. With a somber look on her face, she asked him, "What kind of words are you teaching the kids in your reading clinic?" Tim wondered if the child had noticed some inappropriate words being used in class. In response to his confused expression, the mother clarified her question, saying that she noticed that her child was using words at home that she was not accustomed to hearing her child use, and so she decided to find out what was going on. When we see students using the Tier 2 words from Word Harvests in their own language outside of school, we know they are taking notice of and using the words that will build their vocabulary!

strategy

Games for Skill, Practice, and Extension

What: For our purposes, we divide word games into two categories: a) general/commercial games that are not only fun but also useful in developing a child's interest in words and skill in using them, and b) games that are created or adapted to help students practice specific words they need to learn. Commercial games like Wheel of Fortune, everyday games like Hangman and Ghost, or teacher-inspired games like Hink Pinks fall into the first category. Many different game formats can be adapted to fit the second.

Why: Playing games is basic to human nature and culture. Games pervade our society, from sports to video and computer games to game shows on television. Playing word games and putting word practice into a game format is a way to take advantage of our students' natural interests in playing and their desire to demonstrate their skills and abilities. For students who struggle with literacy, games can improve their motivation for learning, which has often been adversely affected by more traditional activities such as doing workbooks and fill-in-the-blank pages.

Who: Students at any skill level can benefit from playing word games, as long as the materials and tasks fall within their range of ability and therefore provide both a challenge and a reasonable possibility of success. Students can play with other students, friends, parents, and/or teachers.

When and Where: Games can be used for development and practice at various times during the school day. They can serve as a choice activity when students enter the classroom, before formal instruction begins. Many teachers we know have a word game center or station where students can select games to play during free time or when they have completed their work. Some teachers build in a daily or weekly time for games or similar practice activities. In other instances, a teacher might play a game with the whole class to demonstrate a skill, illustrate a point, assess student knowledge, or just for fun! Tutors in our clinics often use word games as a break between challenging activities or as a reward for hard work and focused attention during a demanding session. Struggling students who balk at other reading and writing activities often become absorbed in a game that requires the same skill. Games are also great activities for home practice. Parents can play certain specific games with their children to practice their words. They can also use commercial/general word games for family time activities. Less formal games like Ghost or Hink Pinks can also help to pass the time during car trips. Games can be a means for parents and teachers to fully immerse children in the study of the words that are all around them!

How: You'll find numerous word games available in bookstores, discount stores, and online. Most online games can be played for free on the computer. You can find links to many sites simply by Googling "word games." Each game has its own structure, demands, and skills necessary to be a good player, so you will want to examine each to determine which ones are appropriate for your students. For those you select, you may need to review the rules with your class so that there is no confusion about how the game is played. Some of the procedures involved can be unclear or more complex than the content itself! It is often a good idea to model strategies for success by thinking out loud through an example or turn. For instance, in a letter dice or tile game, you might demonstrate how to organize vowels and consonants or word endings to create as many words as possible or longer words that score higher. You may also consider whether students should play *cooperatively,* either independently or in teams, with the focus on being more successful over time, or *competitively*, one student or team against another. When students collaborate as a team, it's sometimes useful to pair a stronger student with a weaker one, as long as the stronger student doesn't control all the play. When students are competing with each other, it's often a good idea to match individuals and/or teams of comparable ability to keep the game fair.

Board games and the like can easily be adapted to serve as word practice activities. Each team consists of one or more players. You provide each team with its own list of words. Teams exchange lists with the opposing teams, then review the lists together, carefully identifying each word's pronunciation, spelling, structure, and/or meaning, as appropriate to the task. Once the game begins, each team takes its turn, but in order to complete a turn a team must correctly identify, spell, and/ or define one of its words, which the other team presents to them. The winner is determined by whichever team accomplishes the goal of the game first. There are several advantages to this arrangement:

◆ Teams at different ability levels can play against each other because success depends on their learning their own set of words.

◆ The condition that teams only move when members know one of their words provides an important incentive for learning.

- Students learn to examine the words of the opposing side carefully in order to be sure they are correct and therefore allowed to complete their turn. This fosters attention to detail (especially useful for proofreading).

- In the course of play, players often learn their opponent's words as well as their own.

- The element of chance heightens student interest and engagement; though the team that knows its words better may be more likely to win, the results of spinning the wheel or rolling the dice may lead to a different result.

Variations and Extensions: Other game formats lend themselves to word practice as well. For example, your students can play card games like Go Fish, Old Maid or rummy with word cards rather than regular playing cards. Your students can also use word cards in variations of Concentration. Students might also make matches based on word features instead of exact matches, for example, matching two long vowel words or words with the same beginning sound. These can be made easier or harder depending on the abilities of your students. An earlier section provides a full description of a specific example—how bingo can be transformed into WORDO for word practice (pp. 112–115). Teacher-constructed crossword puzzles using student words can also help students brush up on definitions and spelling. Further, you can ask your students to construct the puzzles themselves and try them out on their classmates. Indeed, as you'll discover, there are innumerable ways you can use games and game-like activities to enhance your students' knowledge of words and skills in using them.

The Final Word: Jerry traces the beginning of his own ongoing interest in words to playing simple word games at home. For economic reasons, neither of his parents completed high school. Still, they each had a strong interest in words and language. They routinely tackled the daily and Sunday crossword puzzles in the local paper and played other word games that the paper featured as well. And they drew Jerry and his sister, Betsy, into those games. One of Jerry's earliest memories of family life is sitting around the kitchen table just before dinner time, solving the daily Jumble together (a game in which you unscramble sets of jumbled letters to make real words). Another memory is of playing Ghost to pass the time during vacation travel. (Ghost is a word-building game in which each player adds a letter in sequence. The aim is to avoid being the first to complete a full word. Get forced into completing a word five times and you're a G-H-O-S-T, and out.) Now, whenever he has the opportunity, he enjoys doing those same simple activities with his seven-year-old grandson, Jacob.

Last year over the December holidays, Tim's family was together for the first time in many years. Each evening, the family gathered to play a game before his kids went off with their friends. Later, when Tim and his wife, Kathy, were putting all the games they had played over the week back on the shelf, they were surprised to discover that all the games they had played were, in one form or another, word games. Tim and his family had played Scrabble, Boggle, Balderdash, Wheel of Fortune, Taboo, Quiddler, Bananagrams, Password, Buzzword, and they had even played a few word games from the local newspaper.

Word games are integral to so many of our families' lives. It seems only natural to try to make word study through games an integral part of our classroom lives as well. As we have suggested, there are many ways to put word study into game-like activities. We hope that you have found that many of the activities presented in this book, such as Making and Writing Words, Word Ladders, and WORDO, have this quality, because word study games draw students and keep them engaged in important learning activities. We encourage you to make playing published word study games part of your word study curriculum, to adapt other games to fit word study, and to develop your own games to meet your students' word study needs.

^{In}Conclusion
from the Latin claudere, to close

We hope you have found in these 30 instructional strategies and activities ideas that you can implement in your own classroom. Again, what strategies you choose and the manner in which you implement them is a decision best made by you. Teachers are both scientists and artists. That is why teaching can be such a challenge.

We see one part of teaching as science. The science of word learning tells us that there in no one way to teach words to children. The best that science can offer us is that direct, intensive, engaging, and regular instruction that makes students think deeply about words is what will lead students to a full knowledge of words and how they work. The activities we present in this book are the vehicles that allow you to make word study direct, intensive, engaging, and regular.

Teaching is also an art. In the Introduction, we described the strategies as tools that are part of your word study tool kit. An even better metaphor for the strategies is a palette of colors. If you, the teacher, are an artist (your students are your canvas), then these strategies are the colors on your word study palette. It is up to you to choose and mix the colors that fit best with your style of teaching, your students' style of learning, their developmental needs, and the content you are covering. You are the one who can create that masterpiece in your classroom, so it is up to you now to use these colors (as well as others you may already be using) to create your instructional word study routines that will lead students to deeper levels of knowledge and understanding of words.

Research has shown clearly that children's knowledge of words and spelling develops through stages. Earlier in this book, we noted that the science of word study has taught us that students progress through specific developmental stages as they move from the novice level to maturity in their knowledge of words. As you design your own instruction, please keep in mind your students' level of development.

The science of instruction also tells us that different instructional strategies work better in certain content areas. Again, as you consider the content you wish to cover, think about those strategies that fit best with that content.

The artist in you, however, must also have a say. Consider your own style of teaching, as well as the style of learning that works best for your students. Do you and your students like game-like activities? Is cooperative grouping something that works well in your classroom? Are you a natural storyteller? Do your students need structure and guidance? These are not questions that science can answer; they refer to your own dispositions and those of your students.

Our assumption is that by choosing to read this book, you have committed yourself to making word study part of your instructional experience for you and your students. We hope, then, as you move forward from this book, you will use it as a foundation for developing your own word study program. In the following sections we would like to guide you in taking those next steps in making word study the reality that it needs to be.

Self-Contained Classroom Teachers

As a classroom teacher, you are responsible for the vast majority of what your students learn during the school year. Moreover, since you are most likely working with students in the elementary grades, and since word knowledge is such an important foundation for all learning, we hope that you will consider making word study a separate part of your language arts curriculum—much in the same way that you devote daily instructional time for reading and writing.

Consider the following questions, then, as you move forward:

◆ How much time per day can you give to word study? We hope that you make word study a daily activity and devote a minimum of 15 minutes per day to the study of words—30 minutes would be even better, though we understand the realities of being a teacher.

◆ What will you do with your students during these 15–30 minutes of word study? We suggest you peruse this book once again and choose strategies or activities that you can employ regularly. Choose one or more activities to implement each day of the week.

Jennifer Feeney, a fourth-grade teacher colleague of ours, chose to develop her 30-minute word study curriculum using the following weekly schedule.

- Daily: Devote approximately 15 minutes a day to focused spelling instruction using a modified DSTA approach. Be sure to include Word Sorting and Word Hunting regularly among the activities.

- Daily: Read to students and harvest 5–10 words for the Word Wall. Discuss the words with students and encourage them to use the words in their own oral and written language.

- Mondays: Create a vocabulary antonym-synonym Word Ladder with students. Choose a common word or concept from the thesaurus and have students come up with synonyms or near-synonyms that they then place on the vocabulary timeline on the classroom wall. Throughout the week, students can add words to the chart. At the end of the week, the student with the most entries becomes the following week's Word Wizard.

- Tuesdays: Choose and expand on a Latin or Greek root, one per week. Explain the root and list words that contain the root on a "Classic Word Wall." Encourage students to use and make reference to the words and the root throughout the week. Connect this word to the DSTA spelling activities when possible.

- Wednesdays: Develop a word chart for idioms and other figurative expressions related to a weekly theme and use them throughout the week.

- Thursdays: Play word games with students—Word Ladders, Making and Writing Words, and Word Bingo are among the favorites.

- Fridays: Develop a cloze passage using the words and phrases from the week's Word Walls. Have students read and complete the cloze with words covered during the week.

Alternative: Have students work in pairs to write their own stories or essays using as many words and phrases as possible from the Word Wall. Through their own writing, they will provide evidence that they understand the words studied during the week.

- Students add the words and phrases to their ever-expanding word journals for reference throughout the year.

- As the year progresses, students take on greater responsibility for planning, leading, and implementing these activities on their own.

We absolutely love Jennifer Feeney's word study plan for multiple reasons. First, the activities she has chosen will move students to think deeply about words. Second, the activities are engaging, and their varied nature will keep students interested. Finally, and perhaps most important, Jennifer has, as a teacher-artist, created her own word study curriculum, and so she has embraced her responsibility for her students' learning. She will work hard to ensure that her students benefit from this word study program. Moreover, since she intends to give greater ownership of these activities to her students, she is giving them ownership of the curriculum and making them responsible for their own learning as well. Well done, Jennifer!

Literacy Coaches

Although the concept of reading coach is somewhat new, we have found that reading coaches fill one of the most important roles in any elementary or middle school, that is as leader of professional development in literacy for the faculty. We hope this book has helped you to see the possibilities for sharing the information contained herein with a wider audience. Not only is word study important for teachers of reading and language arts, it is also important for all other content areas. As we have done throughout this book, we ask you to consider the following questions and points:

- What strategies do you think would be most valuable and relevant to all the teachers (special education teachers, content-area teachers, aides and support staff, volunteers, even the clerical and custodial staff) in your building? Which strategies and activities might you share with each of these groups that they would find valuable and reasonable to implement?

- Determine a time and place for presenting the strategies you choose.

- Develop a lesson plan for a quick, informative meeting or set of meetings for presenting the strategies.

◆ Consider how you will follow up with these groups to ensure that they feel comfortable and proficient in the implementation of the strategies.

Word study can no longer be the exclusive province of the language arts or reading teacher. We need to get the message out that anyone who is employed in a school has the opportunity (and the responsibility) to do whatever he or she can to help children become better readers and writers—and one way all of us can make that happen is through some form of word study.

Reading and Language Arts Teachers

At the middle school level, some teachers specialize in teaching reading, writing, and the other language arts. If you are a reading and language arts teacher, we hope that you see word study, even at the middle school level, as a legitimate branch of reading and the language arts. As such, it deserves regular, daily (we hope) instruction and exploration with students, so you need to address some of the same questions that classroom teachers face.

◆ How much time per day can you give to word study, given that you have less than an hour per day with your students?

◆ What activities/strategies would you choose for your word study instruction?

Donna Cooper, a seventh-grade reading/language arts teacher shared with us how she approached word study:

> Fitting word study into my already overloaded curriculum is a tough challenge. However, I recognize that my students' knowledge of words, particularly word meanings, is essential to their ability to read and write well, not to mention their ability to learn in their other subject areas.
>
> I decided to give 15 minutes per day, three days per week, to word study. Rather than do a different activity each day, I thought it would be more profitable to create themes of word study throughout the year. So for the first nine weeks of school we examine how authors use words to make their writing more interesting for readers. We regularly select a set of words from the materials we are reading in our core curriculum.

Then we focus our work on these words. One day we may sort the words using various structural and meaningful categories; another day we find synonyms and antonyms for selected words and post these on our classroom word display. And just like the elementary kids, my students love to play games, so we usually use one day to play a word game.

The second and fourth nine weeks of class, we work on Latin and Greek roots. We choose one or two roots per week. I like to pair Latin and Greek roots with similar meanings, such as *aqua* and *hydro, sub* and *hypo.* We make lists of English words derived from these roots. Then we use the words in our journal writing, and I ask students to "Be the Bard." Students love the freedom of making up new words. Some of the words actually remain on my Word Wall throughout the year. On Fridays, I usually give students a quick quiz over the English words derived from roots. I make the quizzes cumulative so that words learned in previous lessons may also appear in this week's quiz.

I have to admit that I am a bit of "wordaholic." I love words, and I love to think about where words come from. So right after the holidays in the third quarter of class, we do a Word Origins Map and a Word Origins Notebook. Over the years, I have collected several resource books that give the stories of words. I choose three to four words every week, share the stories of the words with students, and have them write responses to the words in the notebooks. The words are also placed on our word display by category, such as words from other languages, acronyms, toponyms, eponyms, heteronyms, and antagonyms. I try to choose words that have interesting stories and that are used by authors in their writing—literary words. It's awfully neat to see not only students' knowledge of words grow, but also their interest in words as well. The proof in the pudding is when you begin to see students using the words you teach them in their own language—it's breathtaking!

It's pretty obvious that our colleague is a lover of words, and she is turning her students into lovers of words as well. We hope that this book will help you and your students also become word lovers!

Content-Area Teachers

As a content-area teacher, you specialize in teaching one or more subject areas. We hope that this book will help you see the need for teaching students about the important words in your own content area and will empower you to try some of these methods with your students. As you move forward, we hope you will consider some of the following questions:

◆ You have your students for a limited time each day, but you need to be committed to word study in your own content area. How much time can you devote to word study per day? Per week?

We suggest that you commit at least five minutes per day (25–30 minutes per week) to the study of words in your content area.

◆ What words should you teach to your students?

We suggest that you peruse the book and other written materials you are using in your classes. Scan the chapters; look through glossaries and indices. Make a list of the words that you feel are critical to your students' understanding of the content you teach. These are the words you should focus on in your teaching.

◆ What methods should you use in your teaching?

Again, you are the artist. Scan this book once again and determine those strategies that you feel best fit the nature of the words you are teaching. Prevoke works well for literature. Possible Sentences is a great strategy for use in science and social studies. Concept Maps and Semantic Feature Analysis are well suited for math, science, and the arts. Word games work well in nearly every subject. Choose three to five strategies that you feel best match your content, your teaching style, and your students. Then commit yourself to using those strategies regularly and consistently.

As you implement each strategy, realize that they will feel clunky, and you may feel awkward at first. However, if you stick with it and allow yourself the freedom to adapt the strategies to your own classroom, you will find that they will become an integral part of your total curriculum. And you will find that students' understanding of the content that you present will improve as well.

Home and Parental Involvement

Just as we regard word study as the responsibility of everyone who works in a school, we also believe that parents and other family members are responsible for helping their children master words at home and beyond. We hope that reading coaches and teachers who have read this book recognize that most of the activities and strategies we present have great potential to foster word learning and are also fairly easy to implement.

We hope, then, that you will feel empowered to share selected strategies from this book with parents. Increasingly, schools are developing ongoing programs in which parents learn simple but effective methods for helping their children learn. The activities in this book are ideal for such a program. Over the course of the year, you and your colleagues could offer monthly, 30-minute mini-workshops to parents, with each workshop focusing on one or two word study strategies.

We understand that parent involvement can be challenging and that to expect every parent to come to every presentation of this sort would be much too optimistic. However, we feel that every long and worthwhile journey begins with a single step. These strategies can be the basis for beginning that journey with parents. If only three parents come to each of your mini-workshops on word study, you will be making an impact on those three families, and in the long term, who can tell where it might lead?

As we conclude, you can no doubt surmise that we are abundantly enthusiastic about word study. In our own lives, the study of words has been interesting and fulfilling. Indeed, we have made, to a large extent, a living from the study of words, but our love of words has also enriched the lives of our families, with whom we have explored words, and the teachers and children with whom we have shared our love of words. Our final hope and wish is that through this book we have imparted to you our love of words so that you may, in turn, do the same for your own students and colleagues. May you, in the same manner as Julius Caesar, end a year of word study with your students and be able to say:

Veni, Vidi, Vici!

I came, I saw, I conquered!

References

Bauman, J. Kame'enui, E., & Ash, G. (2003). Research on vocabulary instruction: Voltaire redux. In J. Flood, D. Lapp, J. Squire, & J. Jenson (Eds.) *Handbook of research on teaching the language arts* (pp. 752–785). Mahwah, NJ: Lawrence Erlbaum.

Beck, I., McKeown, M., & Kucan, L. (2002). *Bringing words to life: Robust vocabulary instruction.* New York: The Guilford Press.

Biemiller, A (in press). *Words worth teaching.* Columbus, OH: SRA/McGraw-Hill.

Birsh, J. R. (2005). *Multisensory teaching of basic language skills* (2nd ed.). Baltimore: Brookes.

Blachowicz, C., & Fisher, P. J. (2002) *Teaching vocabulary in all classrooms* (2nd ed.). Saddle River, NJ: Merrill/Prentice Hall.

Blachowicz, C., & Obrochta, C. (2005) Vocabulary visits: Virtual field trips for content vocabulary development. *The Reading Teacher, 59,* 262–268.

Clements, A. (2003). *Frindle.* New York: Scholastic.

Cunningham, P. M. (2006). High-poverty schools that beat the odds. *The Reading Teacher, 60*(4), 382–385.

Cunningham, P. M (2008). *Phonics they use: Words for reading and writing* (5th ed.). Boston: Allyn & Bacon.

Cunningham, P. M., & Cunningham, J. W. (1992). Making words: Enhancing the spelling-decoding connection. *The Reading Teacher, 46,* 106–115.

Cunningham, P. M., Hall, D. P., & Defee, M. (1998). Nonability groups, multilevel instruction: Eight years later. *The Reading Teacher, 51,* 652–664.

Ehri, L. C., & McCormick, S. (2004). Phases of word learning: Implications for instruction with delayed and disabled readers. In R. B. Ruddell & N. J. Unrau (Eds.), *Theoretical models and processes of reading* (5th ed.), pp. 365–389. Newark, DE: International Reading Association.

Fresch, M. J., & Wheaton, A. (1997). Sort, search, and discover: Spelling in the child-centered classroom. *The Reading Teacher, 51*(1), 20–31.

Fry, E. (1998). The most common phonograms. *The Reading Teacher, 34,* 284–289.

Hart, B., & Risley, T. (1995). *Meaningful differences in the everyday experience of young American children.* Baltimore, MD: Paul H. Brookes Publishing Company.

Invernizzi, M., Abouzeid, M., & Gill, T. (1994). Using students' invented spellings as a guide for spelling instruction that emphasizes word study. *The Elementary School Journal, 95,* (2) 155–167.

Leedy, L., & Street, P. (2003). *There's a frog in my throat: 440 animal sayings a little bird told me.* New York: Holiday House.

McCormick, S., & Zutell, J. (2010). *Instructing students who have literacy problems* (6th ed.). Boston: Pearson/Allyn & Bacon.

Merriam-Webster (2005) *Merriam-Webster's primary dictionary*. Springfield, MA: Merriam-Webster.

National Reading Panel. (2000). *Report of the national reading panel: Teaching children to read: An evidence-based assessment of the scientific research literature on reading and its implications for reading instruction: Report of the subgroups*. Washington, D.C.: U.S. Department of Health and Human Services.

Nagy, W., Herman, P., & Anderson, R. (1985). Learning words from context. *Reading Research Quarterly, 20* (2) 233–253.

Rasinski, T. V. (1994). Developing syntactic sensitivity in reading through phrase-cued texts. *Intervention in School and Clinic, 29*, 165–168.

Rasinski, T. V. (1999a). Making and writing words. *Reading Online*. Retrieved from http://readingonline.org/articles/art_index.asp?HREF=words/index.html

Rasinski, T. V. (1999b). Making and writing words using letter patterns. *Reading Online* Retrieved from http://readingonline.org/articles/art_index.asp?HREF=rasinski/index.html

Rasinski, T. V., & Heym, R. (2008). *Making and writing words—Word families*. Huntington Beach, CA: Shell Educational Publishing.

Rasinski, T., & Padak, N. (2008). *From phonics to fluency: Effective teaching of decoding and reading fluency in the elementary school* (2nd ed.). Boston: Allyn and Bacon.

Rasinski, T. V., Padak, N., Newton, R., & Newton, E. (2008). *Greek and Latin roots: Key to building vocabulary*. Huntington Beach, CA: Shell Educational Publishing.

Scharer, P., & Zutell, J. (2003). The development of spelling. In N. Hall, J. Larson, & J. Marsh (Eds.). *Handbook of early childhood literacy research*. (pp. 77–86); London: Sage.

Stahl, S., & Nagy, W. (2006). *Teaching word meanings*. Mahwah, NJ: Lawrence Erlbaum Associates.

Stauffer, R. G. (1975). *Directing the reading-thinking process*. New York: Harper & Row.

Zutell, J. (1992). An integrated view of word knowledge: Correlational studies of the relationships among spelling, reading, and conceptual development. In S. Templeton, & D. Bear (Eds.). *Development of orthographic knowledge and the foundations of literacy: Memorial festschrift for Edmund H. Henderson*. New York: Lawrence Erlbaum Associates, 213–230.

Zutell, J. (1996). The Directed Spelling Thinking Activity (DSTA): Providing an effective balance in word study instruction. *Reading Teacher, 50, 2*, 98–108.

Zutell, J. (2005). *Word wisdom: Vocabulary for listening, speaking, reading and writing, Levels C–H*. Columbus, OH: Zaner-Bloser Educational Publishers.

Zutell, J., & Rasinski, T. (1989). Reading and spelling connections in third and fifth grade students. *Reading Psychology, 10, 2*, 137–155.

Zutell, J., & Scharer, P. (2007). Using trade books, read-alouds and focused instruction to increase primary-grade students' meaning vocabularies. Paper presented at the 52nd Annual Convention of the International Reading Association, Toronto, Canada, May, 2007.

A list of Additional Professional Readings and Resources on Word Study and Word Play can be found at Tim's website, http://www.timrasinski.com/?page=presentations.

Selected List of Resources:
Word Origins and Expressions

Almond, J. (2000). *Dictionary of word origins: A history of the words, expressions, and clichés we use.* Charleston, SC: Citadel Press. ISBN: 0806517131

Ammer, C. (1992). *Seeing red or tickled pink.* New York, NY: Penguin. ISBN PBK. 0-452-27040-5.

Barnhart, R. (Ed. (1988). *The Barnhart dictionary of etymology.* New York, NY: H. W. Wilson. ISBN 0-8242-0745-9.

Beeler, D. (1988). *Book of roots.* Chicago, IL: Union Representatives. ISBN PBK. 0-918515-00-9.

Davies, P. (1981). *Roots: Family histories of familiar words.* New York, NY: McGraw-Hill. ISBN 0-07-015449-x.

Ehrlich, E. (Ed.). (1990). *The Harper dictionary of foreign terms.* New York, NY: Harper & Row. ISBN 0-06-181576-4.

Funk, C. (2002). *Heavens to Betsy! And other curious sayings. How more than 400 colorful and familiar expressions originated and developed.* New York: Harper. ISBN 0060513314

Hendrickson, R. (1987). *The Henry Holt encyclopedia of word and phrase origins.* New York, NY: Henry Holt. ISBN PBK. 0-8050-1251-6.

Klausner, J. (1990). *Talk about English.* Illustrated by N. Doniger. New York, NY: Thomas Y. Crowell. ISBN TRADE 0-690-04831-9, ISBN LIB. 0-690-04833-5.

Makkai, A. (Ed.). (1987). *A dictionary of American idioms.* New York, NY: Barron's Educational Series. ISBN 0-8120-3899-1.

Mann, L. (1994). *A bird of the hand.* New York, NY: Prentice Hall. ISBN TRADE 0-671-88995-8, ISBN PBK.0-671-88994-x.

Mish, F. C. (Ed.). (1989)). *Webster's word histories.* Springfield, MA: Merriam-Webster.

Rasinski, T., Padak, N., Newton, R, & Newton, E. (2008). *Greek and Latin Roots: Keys to building vocabulary.* Huntington Beach, CA: Shell Educational Publishing. ISBN: 1425804721.

Roget's II: The new thesaurus. (1980). By the editors of the American Heritage Dictionary. Boston, MA: Houghton Mifflin. ISBN 0-395-29605-6.

Smith, C., & Reade, E. (1994). *Word history: A resource book for the teacher.* Bloomington, IN: ERIC Clearinghouse on Reading and Communication Skills. ISBN 0-927516-44-6.

Smith, C. B., & Reade, E. W. (1991). Word history: A guide to understanding the English language. Bloomington, IN: ERIC Clearinghouse on Reading and Communication Skills. ISBN PBK. 0-927516-12-8.

A more extensive list, Additional Professional Readings and Resources on Word Study and Word Play, can be found at Tim's website, http://www.timrasinski.com/?page=presentations.

Making and Writing Words *Response Form, Grades 2+*

Vowels	Consonants

1	6	11
2	7	12
3	8	13
4	9	14
5	10	15

Transfer

T–1	T–2	T–3
T–4	T–5	T–6

Making and Writing Words *Response Form, Primary Grades*

Vowels	Consonants
1	**5**
2	**6**
3	**7**
4	**8**

Transfer

T–1	**T–2**
T–3	**T–4**

Essential Strategies for Word Study | **Appendix**